T0295945

Monetary Policy and Food Inflation in Emerging and Developing Economies

This book focuses on the impact of monetary policy and food price volatility and inflation in emerging and developing economies.

The tendency for food price volatility to blot inflation forecasting accuracy, engender tail dynamics in the overall inflation trajectory and derail economic welfare is well known in the literature. The ability of monetary policy to exact stability in food prices, theoretically, has also been well espoused. The empirical evidence, however, is not only in short supply, but also the studies available have dwelt on approaches that underplay the volatile behaviour of food prices. This book focuses on inflation targeting in emerging economies such as Chile, Mexico, Turkey, Brazil, Hungary, Russia, Colombia, South Africa, Indonesia and Ghana, as these are economies with considerable proportion of the consumption basket occupied by food. This book provides the means to understand at first hand the correct way to model food inflation, account for the related policy responses to deviations either in the short or medium to long term, and in market conditions that are subject to excessive variability. Strong evidence is presented that captures deviations of food prices from their trend and the accompanying monetary policy effect in stabilizing such variabilities across distinct frequencies. The novel approach in this book addresses the burgeoning puzzles of asymmetry in monetary policy effect on food prices at high, medium and low episodes of food inflation. In doing so, this book presents a powerful tool for researchers interested in understanding not just the transmission mechanism, but also the magnitudes involved, and to policymakers whose existing tools have failed them. Future studies will do well to deepen the evidence and seek new grounds to which the phenomenon manifests beyond and below emerging markets.

This book will be of great interest to students, scholars and policy-makers involved in agricultural economics, financial economics, food security and sustainable development.

Abdul-Aziz Iddrisu is a senior lecturer in the Department of Banking Technology and Finance at Kumasi Technical University, Ghana.

Imhotep Paul Alagidede is a metaeconomist at the Nile Valley Multiversity, and professor of Finance at the University of the Witwatersrand, South Africa, and SDD-UBIDS at Wa, Ghana.

Routledge Focus on Environment and Sustainability

Sustainability in High-Excellence Italian Food and Wine
Laura Onofri

Learning to Live with Climate Change
From Anxiety to Transformation
Blanche Verlie

Social Innovation in the Service of Social and Ecological Transformation
The Rise of the Enabling State
Olivier De Schutter and Tom Dedeurwaerdere

Gender, Food and COVID-19
Global Stories of Harm and Hope
Edited by Paige Castellanos, Carolyn E. Sachs and Ann R. Tickamyer

Natural Resource Leadership and Management
A Practical Guide for Professionals
Frederick Cubbage

Monetary Policy and Food Inflation in Emerging and Developing Economies
Abdul-Aziz Iddrisu and Imhotep Paul Alagidede

Mathematical Models and Environmental Change
Case Studies in Long Term Management
Douglas J. Crookes

For more information about this series, please visit: www.routledge.com/
Routledge-Focus-on-Environment-and-Sustainability/book-series/RFES

Monetary Policy and Food Inflation in Emerging and Developing Economies

Abdul-Aziz Iddrisu and Imhotep Paul Alagidede

LONDON AND NEW YORK

First published 2022
by Routledge
2 Park Square, Milton Park, Abingdon, Oxon OX14 4RN

and by Routledge
605 Third Avenue, New York, NY 10158

Routledge is an imprint of the Taylor & Francis Group, an informa business

© 2022 Abdul-Aziz Iddrisu and Imhotep Paul Alagidede

The right of Abdul-Aziz Iddrisu and Imhotep Paul Alagidede to be identified as authors of this work has been asserted in accordance with sections 77 and 78 of the Copyright, Designs and Patents Act 1988.

British Library Cataloguing-in-Publication Data
A catalogue record for this book is available from the British Library

Library of Congress Cataloging-in-Publication Data
Names: Iddrisu, Abdul-Aziz, author. | Alagidede, Paul, author.
Title: Monetary policy and food inflation in emerging and developing economies / Abdul-Aziz Iddrisu and Imhotep Paul Alagidede.
Description: New York, NY : Routledge, 2022. | Series: Routledge focus on environment and sustainability | Includes bibliographical references and index.
Identifiers: LCCN 2021037552 (print) | LCCN 2021037553 (ebook) | ISBN 9781032049663 (hardback) | ISBN 9781032049694 (paperback) | ISBN 9781003195368 (ebook)
Subjects: LCSH: Monetary policy--Developing countries. | Food prices--Developing countries. | Inflation (Finance)-- Developing countries.
Classification: LCC HG1496 .I23 2022 (print) | LCC HG1496 (ebook) | DDC 332.109172/4--dc23
LC record available at https://lccn.loc.gov/2021037552
LC ebook record available at https://lccn.loc.gov/2021037553

ISBN: 978-1-032-04966-3 (hbk)
ISBN: 978-1-032-04969-4 (pbk)
ISBN: 978-1-003-19536-8 (ebk)

DOI: 10.4324/9781003195368

Typeset in Times New Roman
by MPS Limited, Dehradun

Contents

Figures

Tables

Preface

The tendency for food price volatility to blot inflation forecasting accuracy, engender tail dynamics in the overall inflation trajectory and derail economic welfare is well known in the literature. The ability of monetary policy to exact stability in food prices, theoretically, has been well espoused. The empirical evidence, however, is not only in short supply, but also limited studies have dwelled on approaches that completely ignore the volatile behaviour of food prices. This variability is extreme in economies that are now embracing free-market economic programmes and policies and emerging and developing economies with substantial food dominance in the consumption baskets. The lack of understanding of how food inflation heightens and/or dampens inflation variability and the pass-through of policy to food prices and vice versa is partly to account for the halfhearted response of monetary policy to many economic aggregates. There is the need to close this gap and illuminate the subject because it is such variabilities in food prices that make them ruinous to the effective conduct of monetary policy, inflation forecasting accuracy and welfare subtleties. This book focuses on inflation targeting emerging and developing economies such as Chile, Mexico, Turkey, Brazil, Hungary, Russia, Colombia, South Africa, Indonesia and Ghana, as these are economies with considerable proportion of the consumption basket occupied by food. The methodological weaknesses of previous studies are addressed in this book by appealing to models that decompose food inflation from emerging and developing economies settings into various frequencies and horizons, while allowing for the conditional median response of food inflation to a variety of monetary policy tools. The results show that the effect of monetary policy on food prices for the selected countries is mixed. While monetary policy exerts positive impact on food prices over different horizons and distinct quantiles in Brazil,

Chile, Ghana, Hungary, Mexico, Russia, South Africa and Turkey, its effect on food prices in Colombia and Indonesia is mixed. The results in these two countries differ across scales and quantiles. In Colombia, monetary policy delivers stability on food prices only over the short horizon (two-to-four-month horizon). At long horizons, monetary policy restrictions engender destabilization in food prices. For Brazil, Chile, Ghana, Hungary, Mexico, Russia, South Africa and Turkey, monetary and fiscal policies necessarily have to be complementary given the positive monetary policy-food inflation nexus. In Colombia and Indonesia, the involvement of fiscal authorities may not be necessary. Monetary policy authorities can exact stability in food prices over the short-to-medium horizons. A comprehension of the transmission dynamics and timing as well as a reasonably accurate forecast of the path of food prices would be critical for these countries. This book would be beneficial to monetary and fiscal authorities of emerging and developing economies, academics in macroeconomics, think tanks in the field of monetary economics, postgraduate students in macroeconomics and would be an invaluable reference for studies on monetary policy-food inflation nexus.

Keywords: Food inflation; monetary policy; emerging and developing economies; inflation targeting.

1 Introduction and background to the study

Introduction

The dominant role of food prices in driving overall price levels (Iddrisu & Alagidede, 2020; Ginn & Pourroy, 2020); their volatility and persistence that dent inflation forecasting accuracy (Ginn & Pourroy, 2020; Alper et al., 2016; Portillo et al., 2016) and the associated uncertainty in the conduct of monetary policy (Ginn & Pourroy, 2020) are well known in the theoretical and empirical literature. These characteristics are even more pronounced in emerging and developing economies in view of the dominance of food in the consumption baskets of these economies, thereby making optimal conduct of inflation targeting framework a major challenge (see Iddrisu & Alagidede, 2020). Unsurprisingly, many emerging inflation targeting economies have struggled to achieve publicly announced inflation targets over the years and this can affect the credibility of policymakers.

Whether monetary policy exacts stability in food prices, as espoused by the theoretical literature (Ginn & Pourroy, 2020; Pourroy et al., 2016; Catao & Chang, 2015), is an important empirical question that has received little attention in the literature. So far, studies on this subject have focused largely on monetary policy and overall inflation to the neglect of food price stability. Much as some attempts have been made recently in the literature (Iddrisu & Alagidede, 2021; Iddrisu & Alagidede, 2020; Bhattacharya & Jain, 2020; Hammoudeh et al., 2015), fundamental limitations still linger. What makes food prices a major concern for monetary policy authorities is its underlying variability that minimises the accuracy of inflation forecasts; breeds uncertainty in the conduct of monetary policy; destabilise planning and income of farmers/producers and derail economic welfare for the poor in particular. Surprisingly, existing studies, save Iddrisu & Alagidede (2021, 2020), have tended to use models that completely ignore this all-important

DOI: 10.4324/9781003195368-1

characteristic of food prices. Although Iddrisu & Alagidede (2021, 2020) employed the quantile regression analysis that captures tail dynamics resulting from outliers in food prices, such an approach fails to address the frequency of food price changes and deviations from the trend that are even more ruinous to inflation forecasting accuracy and engenders uncertainties in the conduct of monetary policy.

Importantly, all the existing studies have been situated exclusively in time domain, ignoring the fact that economic agents have distinct objectives over distinct horizons and frequencies. This obvious mishap was highlighted by Aguiar-Conraria et al. (2008), who posit that the actions of different economic agents are informed by different objectives across distinct horizons which eventually underlie numerous economic processes. The resulting macroeconomic data that are observed are essentially a crystallisation of these distinct economic agents' objectives and horizons. To examine monetary policy effect on food prices in an exclusive time domain is to obscure the underlying distinct objectives and horizons of economic agents. Indeed, Aguiar-Conraria et al. (2018) argued that monetary policy affects over distinct horizons and especially cyclical frequencies are crucial for policymakers, given the distinct impact on social welfare over these different frequencies.

This book overcomes these limitations in the literature by adopting an approach that situates the monetary policy–food inflation nexus in time and frequency domains. It employs the wavelet-based quantile regressions to capture deviations of food prices from their trend and the accompanying monetary policy effect in stabilising such variabilities across distinct frequencies over time. The application of the quantile regression then gives the added advantage of capturing monetary policy effect on food prices at high, medium and low episodes of food inflation. This further illuminates the well-acknowledged asymmetry in monetary policy behaviour as discussed by Iddrisu & Alagidede (2021, 2020).

The focus of this book is on emerging and developing economies that have large proportions of food in their consumption baskets and high levels of indigence in their economies. Pourroy et al. (2016) reckon that 50% of the budget of households in developing countries is allocated to food alone. Specifically, the focus on inflation targeting economies such as Chile, Mexico, Turkey, Brazil, Hungary, Russia, Colombia, South Africa, Indonesia and Ghana brings into sharp focus, the several dynamics of inflation targeting such as the central role played by volatile food prices that distorts forecasting accuracy of inflation and highlights the essential toolkits of inflation targeting for inclusion in the tool boxes of central banks. The uncertainties that come with such variabilities present enormous concerns for monetary policymakers in exacting optimal policy. As a result, central banks that target inflation place significant importance on food price developments.

The findings show that the effect of monetary policy on food prices for the selected countries is mixed. While monetary policy exerts a positive impact on food prices over different horizons and distinct quantiles in Brazil, Chile, Ghana, Hungary, Mexico, Russia, South Africa and Turkey, its effect on food prices in Colombia and Indonesia is inconclusive. The results in these two countries differ across scales and quantiles. In Colombia, monetary policy delivers stability on food prices only over the short horizon of two to four months. At longer horizons, the effect of monetary policy on food prices in Colombia is positive. For Indonesia, food price stability is exacted by monetary policy over the short to medium horizon. At the longer horizon, monetary policy restriction engenders destabilization in food prices.

Overview of the book

This book takes a careful look at the concept of inflation targeting and its preconditions. It looks at the experiences of the aforementioned emerging and developing economies since their respective adoption of the inflation targeting framework. The book considers the inflation performance of these countries prior and post inflation targeting. The inflation targets that are publicly announced in these countries and how the respective central banks have achieved these targets are examined from a fresh perspective, while the developments in world food prices and the dynamics and trajectories of food inflation in the selected countries vis-à-vis the overall inflation are brought into sharp focus. The co-movements of food and overall prices, the volatilities and persistence, as well as the implications of the underlying volatilities and persistence of food inflation for the conduct of monetary policy in emerging and developing economies are given a new space for broader discussion. Finally, the book delves into the more empirical matters of the monetary policy effect on food prices using wavelet-based quantile regressions and proffer a variety of options for policy.

Structure of the book

This book is organised into five chapters as follows:

Chapter 1 provides a brief overview and structure of the book.

Chapter 2 looks at inflation performance, milestones and challenges under the inflation targeting framework in the selected countries. It then compares these outcomes to the performance of inflation prior to the adoption of the targeting framework in each of these countries. In doing so, the chapter also compares actual inflation outturn to the publicly announced inflation targets in these countries.

Chapter 3 examines the developments in world food prices and the movements in food and overall inflation in the selected countries. It examines the volatilities and persistence in food inflation and the implication for inflation forecasting and conduct of monetary policy in the selected countries.

Chapter 4 estimates monetary policy effect on food prices in time and frequency domains using the wavelet-based quantile regression approach. This chapter undertakes robustness cheques and discusses the policy ramifications of the results.

Chapter 5 presents the summary of the journey and explores areas where future research on the topic could yield the greatest reward.

References

Aguiar-Conraria, L., Azevedo, N., & Soares, M. J. (2008). Using wavelets to decompose the time–frequency effects of monetary policy. *Physica A: Statistical Mechanics and its Applications, 387*(12), 2863–2878.

Aguiar-Conraria, L., Martins, M. M., & Soares, M. J. (2018). Estimating the Taylor rule in the time-frequency domain. *Journal of Macroeconomics, 57*, 122–137.

Alper, C. E., Hobdari, N., & Uppal, A. (2016). Food inflation in Sub-Saharan Africa: Causes and Policy Implications. *IMF Working Paper*. WP/16/247.

Bhattacharya, R., & Jain, R. (2020). Can monetary policy stabilise food inflation? Evidence from advanced and emerging economies. *Economic Modelling, 89*, 122–141.

Catao, L. A., & Chang, R. (2015). World food prices and monetary policy. *Journal of Monetary Economics 75*, 69–88.

Ginn, W., & Pourroy, M. (2020). Should a central bank react to food inflation? Evidence from an estimated model for Chile. *Economic Modelling, 90*, 221–234.

Hammoudeh, S., Nguyen, D. K., & Sousa, R. M. (2015). US monetary policy and sectoral commodity prices. *Journal of International Money and Finance, 57*, 61–85.

Iddrisu, A. A., & Alagidede, I. P. (2020). Monetary policy and food inflation in South Africa: A quantile regression analysis. *Food Policy, 91*, 101816.

Iddrisu, A. A., & Alagidede, I. P. (2021). Asymmetry in food price responses to monetary policy: A quantile regression approach. *SN Business and Economics, 1*, 52.

Portillo, R., Zanna, L. P., O'Connell, S., & Peck, R. (2016). Implications of food subsistence for monetary policy and inflation. *IMF Working Paper*, WP/16/70.

Pourroy, M., Carton, B., & Coulibaly, D. (2016). Food prices and inflation targeting in emerging economies. *International Economics*, *146*, 108–140.

2 Inflation targeting framework in emerging and developing economies: Experiences and milestones

Introduction

The inflationary episodes of the 1970s and parts of 1980s that struck a number of advanced economies prompted a transition to inflation targeting framework by these countries as monetary policy strategies such as the monetary targeting and pegged exchange rate regimes could not deliver the needed price stability (Svensson, 2011). Masson et al. (1997) reckon that the challenges of monetary targeting and pegged exchange rate regimes in the 1990s precipitated an exodus to inflation targeting framework by a number of advanced economies as a way to improve their inflation footprint. New Zealand was the first nation to unveil inflation targeting framework in the world in the year 1990. Other advanced countries followed, with Canada unveiling the framework in 1991, the United Kingdom in 1992, Australia in 1993 and Sweden in 1995. What the inflation targeting framework embodies and the foundations that define its successful implementation or otherwise are the subject of the succeeding sections of this chapter.

The nature and pre-requisites of inflation targeting

The inflation targeting framework involves public communication of a quantitative inflation target by a central bank, to which it exercises commitment and strives to achieve in order to establish credibility and anchor inflation expectations. The framework also embodies transparency and engender accountability as monetary policy authorities regularly engage the public on decisions arrived at and the factors that informed the said decisions. Such transparency and public engagements help to shape the inflation expectations of the public in a way that engender convergence to the announced inflation target.

The numerical or quantitative inflation target can be a range, a point target with or without a tolerance band (Svensson, 2011). For instance,

DOI: 10.4324/9781003195368-2

South Africa has an inflation target range of 3%–6%; Ghana has a point target of 8% with a tolerance band of 2% (thus 8% ± 2%) and the United Kingdom has a point target of 2% without a tolerance band. Hungary had previously used a point target of 3% but has, since 2015, added a tolerance band of 1%. The inflation target may be determined by the monetary policy authorities or the fiscal authorities or both. For instance, while the inflation target is set jointly by the fiscal authorities and the central bank in Ghana, it is determined by the fiscal authorities in South Africa. Meanwhile, the central bank sets the inflation target in Peru.

Carare & Stone (2003) categorise inflation targeting into regimes on the basis of central bank credibility and clarity in respect of commitment to the publicly announced inflation target. The central bank's credibility is determined by the achievement or otherwise of the announced inflation target, while clarity is ascertained by the target inflation announcement and the institutional mechanisms designed to foster accountability on the publicly announced target. The regimes include full-fledged inflation targeting, eclectic inflation targeting and inflation targeting lite. Countries that practice inflation targeting lite are deemed to have minimal credibility and therefore communicate a broader objective for inflation without committing to a specific quantitative target nor pursue inflation as the primary goal of the central bank. These countries grapple with weak institutional setup, unstable financial system and significant susceptibility to major economic shocks. The full-fledged inflation targeting countries, on the other hand, possess relatively high credibility, with commitment to delivering the publicly announced inflation target and pursuing stable prices as the primary objective of the central bank. They put in place institutional mechanisms that reinforce their commitment to the inflation target and engender accountability and transparency in the process. Countries that are into eclectic inflation targeting are deemed to have substantial credibility and track record of delivering low and stable prices to the extent that they do not have to showcase measures of accountability and transparency. With such credibility levels and ability to churn out low and stable prices, these countries have the latitude to pursue the dual objective of price and output stability (Carare & Stone, 2003).

Literature acknowledges the fact that inflation targeting framework, like any other monetary policy strategies, thrives on the presence of a number of preconditions. Masson et al. (1997) outline the prerequisites for successful implementation of the inflation targeting regime as the independence of monetary policy authorities to conduct monetary policy devoid of fiscal interference; and sole commitment to inflation target without focusing on any other variables as nominal anchor. According to Mishkin (2000), the fundamental pillars of the inflation targeting framework include numerical inflation targets announced publicly; the fundamental goal and preoccupation of monetary policy authorities is the achievement of price stability with unwavering institutional commitment; an information-rich approach involving the deployment of numerous variables in the determination of instruments for monetary policy; public-engaging strategy involving frequent communication of decisions and objectives of monetary policy authorities to the market and the wider public to engender transparency; and accountability of monetary policy authorities on the achievement of the publicly announced inflation target.

Furthermore, Schaechter et al. (2000) outlined key success factors for the implementation of inflation targeting framework as follows: established macroeconomic stability and robust fiscal position; sophisticated financial system; a clear price stability mandate for the central bank along with independence for determining monetary policy instruments; succinct appreciation of the link between inflation and instruments for monetary policy; robust techniques for delivering forecasts of inflation; and measures for enhancing credibility and accountability. For Batini & Laxton (2007), the preconditions for a successful inflation targeting framework implementation are the autonomy of the central bank and freedom from political and fiscal authorities to avert deviations from the objective of price stability; well-established technical infrastructure with competence in forecasting inflation and modelling that are supported by data availability; absence of regulated prices, minimal dollarization and less susceptibility to changes in exchange rate and commodity prices; and a robust financial system with sophisticated capital markets and banking institutions. Svensson (2011) adds inflation forecasting as a key pillar in the inflation targeting implementation. The author also reckons that at the heart of the framework are three key factors: the mandate of price stability; accountability of monetary policy authorities and the independence of the authorities charged with the responsibility of monetary policy decisions.

These pre-requisites and success factors of inflation targeting framework bear the footprints of advanced economy features as the framework emanated from that context. However, the inflation targeting framework enjoyed acceptance and adoption beyond the advanced economy context to developing and emerging market countries. Meanwhile, the economic architecture of these contexts (advanced versus emerging and developing economies) necessarily differs. Whether these pre-requisites must necessarily be present in the emerging and developing economies and how inflation targeting framework was born in these countries are the subject of the next sections.

Inflation targeting framework in the context of emerging and developing economies

The relative success of inflation targeting framework in the context of advanced economies endeared it to a number of emerging market countries which were emerging from financial debacle of the 1990s occasioned by the pitfalls of the regimes of pegged exchange rate (Mishkin, 2000). However, the requirements of autonomy of central banks, technical competences and robust financial systems for successful enactment of the inflation targeting regime prompted the argument in the literature that the framework is unsuitable for emerging market economies as these preconditions are virtually nonexistent in these countries (Svensson, 2011). On the basis of a survey of emerging market inflation targeting countries, however, Batini & Laxton (2007) had observed that none of the surveyed inflation targeting emerging market countries possessed the aforementioned preconditions, leading the authors to argue that the success or otherwise of the inflation targeting framework implementation is not predicated on the presence of these conditions. The implication of the outcome of the survey is to the effect that the prescribed preconditions are not cast in stone and that the economic realities of different economies are even more germane. Some of the early emerging market economies to embrace inflation targeting framework in the 1990s include Israel, Chile, Brazil and Colombia. Other emerging market economies such as South Africa, Mexico, Hungary, Peru, Indonesia and Turkey followed later. The experiences of some of these emerging markets and developing economies such as Brazil, Chile, Colombia, Ghana, Hungary, Indonesia, Mexico, Russia, South Africa and Turkey are considered in the subsequent section.

Brazil

Unlike the other emerging market economies that phased in inflation targeting framework steadily, Brazil quickened the announcement and implementation of the inflation targeting framework over a short period of time (Libânio, 2010). The country proclaimed the intention to adopt inflation targeting framework in March 1999 and by July 1999, it had officially unveiled the framework following an enactment of Decree No. 3,088 in June 1999 that laid the foundation for the official unveiling of the framework (Banco Central Do Brasil, 2016). The country was beset by the challenges of the pegged exchanged rate regime and rising inflation. The floating exchange rate regime was embraced and inflation targeting framework was deemed an ideal monetary policy strategy that fits the flexible exchange rate proposition (Libânio, 2010). Brazil launched inflation targeting framework in 1999 under a Presidential decree no. 3088, with inflation target first set at 8% along with a tolerance band of 2%. Thus, actual inflation was allowed to fluctuate between 6% and 10%. The targets have varied over the years, informed by economic realities. The targets for the years 2021 and 2022 are 3.75% and 3.5%, respectively, with a tolerance band of 1.5%. The inflation target is set by the National Monetary Council. The monetary policy instrument in Brazil is called *Selic*, a rate applicable on daily interbank borrowings. The monetary policy committee (MPC), also known as the *Copom*, determines the *Selic* rate every 45 days or eight times in a year.

Chile

The use of exchange rate as an anchor to provide stability in the price levels was very popular in Chile, especially in the late 1950s, early 1960s and between the end of 1970s and early 1980s. The abysmal failure of the exchange rate regime in exacting the needed stability brought to fore the need for the central bank of Chile to embrace an alternative monetary policy strategy. Given the instability in money demand and the feeble financial system, monetary aggregates were considered to be unsuitable intermediate targets in delivering stability. The inflation targeting framework emerged as the obvious choice for the central bank in its attempts to engender stability (Morandé & Schmidt-Hebbel, 2000). Partial inflation targeting started in September 1990, although full-fledged inflation targeting framework was unveiled in September 1999. The central bank has a two-year inflation target horizon, with a point estimate target of 3% but actual inflation can be allowed to fluctuate between 2% and 4% tolerance band. The monetary policy instrument is the monetary policy rate which is determined by the central bank's Board. The Board determines the policy rates at meetings that are held eight times per annum, with dates predetermined and announced in the prior year. Meanwhile, emergency meetings can be called as circumstances may dictate. The policy rate is arrived at by the Board based on informed votes by members.

Colombia

Colombia, prior to the adoption of inflation targeting framework, had crawling peg exchange rate regime along with the control of monetary aggregates. The instability of the capital flows in the 1990s along with the difficulty in managing monetary aggregates occasioned by the exchange rate regime prompted the country to turn to inflation targeting regime and allow the exchange rate to float. The preparation towards the adoption of the inflation targeting regime started in 1991, with the granting of autonomy to the board of the country's central bank by the constitution. The board of the central bank was then authorised, in 1992, to announce annual targets for inflation (Hamann et al., 2014). The inflation targeting framework in Colombia was launched in 1999 with a target of 3% and a tolerance band of 1%. The monetary policy instrument used by the central bank is the benchmark interest rate or intervention rate or monetary policy interest rate. The central bank's Board takes monetary policy decisions at eight meetings per annum meant to guide inflation expectations to the target.

Ghana

Ghana, prior to the adoption of inflation targeting framework, was practicing monetary targeting framework. The instability in demand for money in the 1990s (Bawumia et al., 2008), meant that the monetary targeting regime failed to deliver the primary objective of price stability. The high inflation levels over that period led Ghana to initiate a transition to inflation targeting framework which was eventually unveiled in 2007. The target inflation rate set for that year (2007) was in a range of 7%–9%. In addition, a medium-term (two years) target of 5% was set in 2007. Since 2015, the medium-term target inflation in Ghana has been 8% along with a tolerance band of 2%, with this target determined by both the Bank of Ghana and the government. The MPC is vested with the power to make monetary policy decisions by setting the monetary policy rate determined at meetings held every two months.

Hungary

Inflation rates in Hungary, prior to 2001, were in the double-digit zone and coincided with a period when the country was using the crawling peg exchange rate regime (Erdös, 2008). The inflation targeting framework was implemented in June 2001 with a target of 7% set for the year and 4.5% set for the following year (2002). In December 2001, a target of 3.5% was set for the year 2003. Subsequent targets of 3.5%, 4% and 3.5% were set for 2004, 2005 and 2006, respectively, with each of these targets determined two years prior to the reference year. A medium-term inflation target of 3% was set in August 2005 and remained so until March 2015 when a tolerance band of 1% was added to the 3%. Thus, actual inflation can fluctuate between 2% and 4% since March 2015. Monetary policy instrument, known as the monetary policy rate, is determined by the Monetary Council on a monthly basis through voting.

Indonesia

With a reputation of high inflation rates over the years, particularly in the 1960s and to some extent in the 1990s when the Asian financial crisis devastated most emerging market economies, the central bank of Indonesia adopted base money targeting after deserting the regime of crawling exchange rate band in 1997. The country's legislature, through regulatory enactment in 1999, granted autonomy to the central bank and explicitly determined the objectives of the central bank (Kenward, 2013). This regulatory development precipitated significant shifts in monetary policy conduct and laid the foundation for the eventual transition to the current inflation targeting framework (Alamsyah et al., 2001). The country adopted inflation targeting framework in 2005, with inflation targets set by the government and not the central bank. However, the monetary policy rate, used to guide inflation to the announced target, is determined by the Board of Governors of the central bank. The Board determines the policy rate every month. The current inflation target is 3% with a 1% inflation tolerance band.

Mexico

The exchange rate challenges of the 1990s in Mexico and the accompanying crisis saw a transition from a regime of exchange rate target zone to a flexible exchange rate regime. The inflationary experience in the crisis period necessitated a policy shift to inflation targeting framework (Ramos-Francia & Garcia, 2005). The adoption of inflation targeting framework was heralded by the review of the laws of the country's central bank in 1993. The said review established the autonomy of the central bank and set the pace for the eventual adoption of the inflation targeting framework in 1999 (Carrasco & Ferreiro,

2013). Inflation targeting framework was launched in 2001 in Mexico, with the inflation target set by the central bank's Board of Governors. The Board also determines the monetary policy instrument, known as the overnight interbank rate, on the basis of consensus. The Board meets eight times in a year to set these rates. The medium-term inflation target is currently 3% with a tolerance band of 1%.

Russia

Inflation targeting framework in Russia was unveiled in 2007, with the power to make monetary policy decisions vested in the Board of Directors. The annual inflation target is 4%. Monetary policy instrument designed to achieve this target is called *key rate* in Russia and is set by the Board of Directors at eight meetings which are held every year. Four of these meetings are known as core meetings which are held every quarter. The remaining four meetings are known as interim meetings held in between the four main quarters of the year. Monetary policy decisions are arrived at through consensus.

South Africa

The targeting of growth of monetary aggregates preceded inflation targeting framework in South Africa. The disconnection between inflation and monetary aggregates rendered monetary targeting strategy undesirable in keeping low and stable prices in the country. As a result, inflation targeting framework was launched in February 2000, with a target range of 3%–6% determined by the government. It is the first African country to embrace full-fledged inflation targeting framework. The monetary policy instrument is the *repo rate* set by the Reserve Bank's MPC at meetings held at least every two months or a minimum of six times per annum.

Turkey

The country's prolonged inflationary past, exacerbated by the weakening lira, prompted a transition from the orthodox monetary policy to the adoption of inflation targeting framework in Turkey (Genc & Balcilar, 2012). Implicit inflation targeting started in Turkey in 2002 and lasted until 2005. A formal launch of the inflation targeting framework took place in 2006. The inflation target is set by the central bank and the fiscal authorities. Since 2012, inflation target has been set at 5% with a tolerance band of 2%. Monetary policy decisions, designed to achieve the target, are taken by the MPC which currently meets eight times per annum. The MPC previously met every month. Monetary policy decisions are arrived at through voting.

Following implementation of inflation targeting in the emerging and developing economies, the natural question is whether these countries have chalked the successes that the framework delivered in the advanced economies. The answer to this is the preoccupation of the next section.

A comparative analysis of inflation performance prior and post adoption of inflation targeting framework

This section looks at inflation performance prior and post adoption of inflation targeting framework in the selected emerging market and developing economies. The analysis is multi-layered. For each country, a comparison is made of its inflation levels before and after inflation targeting framework adoption. Given that the essence of inflation targeting framework is not only to achieve low but also stable inflation levels, this section also looks at the variations in observed inflation levels prior and post inflation targeting adoption. It then compares, in the post inflation targeting adoption period, the actual inflation against the publicly announced inflation targets. In doing all these analyses, this section relies on annual inflation rate data from the World Bank's World Development Indicators (WDI).

Brazil

Prior to the launch of inflation targeting framework in Brazil in 1999, inflation in Brazil was endemic, particularly in the late 1980s and most of the 1990s, averaging 645.46% between 1981 and 1998 and peaking at 2947.73% in 1990. Post-inflation targeting adoption, inflation rates fell sharply to an average of 6.73% between 1999 and 2016. By 2019, inflation rate had reached 3.73%. The adoption of inflation targeting framework in Brazil, as per Table 2.1 and Figure 2.1, appears to have delivered relatively low prices compared to the previous monetary policy regimes.

The essence of inflation targeting framework is not only about the achievement of low inflation rates but also stable prices. Relying on coefficient of variation, a comparison is made of the extent of stability or variability in the observed prices before and over the inflation targeting period. As per Table 2.1, the period before inflation targeting adoption was not only inflationary but also exhibited significant

Table 2.1 Descriptive statistics on inflation rate in Brazil

	Before Inflation Targeting	*Inflation Targeting Period*
Mean	645.46	6.73
Maximum	2947.73	14.72
Minimum	3.20	3.64
Standard Deviation	872.97	2.49
Coefficient of Variation	1.35	0.37
Number of Observations	18	18

Note: The WDI annual inflation rate data on Brazil starts from 1981. This provides 18 observations for the period prior to inflation targeting adoption. For comparison, 18 observations are used for the inflation targeting period too. Thus, from 1999 to 2016. Same reasoning is applied to the other countries such that observations prior and post inflation targeting adoption are matched on the basis of data availability or the date of start of inflation targeting regime to make a meaningful comparison.

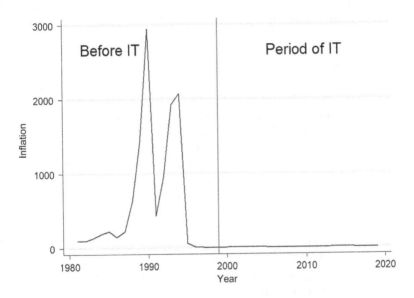

Figure 2.1 Inflation before and during Inflation Targeting (IT) in Brazil.

variability with coefficient of variation of 1.35 compared to 0.37 for the period of inflation targeting, an indication that the inflation targeting framework in Brazil witnessed low and stable prices.

Much as inflation has been relatively low and stable in the inflation targeting period, a bigger question relating to the credibility of the central bank is whether the publicly announced inflation targets were met. In 1999 when inflation targeting started, inflation stood at 4.86%, well below the midpoint target of 8%. The target was reviewed downwards to 6% in the following year with a 2% tolerance band. Actual inflation stood at 7.04% in that year, exceeding the midpoint target of 6% but within the tolerance band of 4%–8%. In 2002, the inflation target was reviewed further downwards to 3.5% along with a tolerance of 2%. Meanwhile, actual inflation stood at 8.45%, breaching the upper limit of the tolerance band of 1.5%–5.5%. Inflation target for 2003 was initially set at 3.25% with a tolerance band of 2% but was later revised upwards to 4% along with a tolerance band of 2.5%. Interestingly, actual inflation for the year was 14.71% which is more than double the upper limit of the inflation tolerance band of 1.5%–6.5%. It was revised from an initial 3.75% with a tolerance band of 2.5% to a new target of 5.5% with a tolerance band of 2.5%. So in effect, the tolerance band remained the same but the base target was changed from 3.75% to 5.5%. Actual inflation of 6.6% for the year breached the revised midpoint target of 5.5% but was within the inflation tolerance band. In 2005, the inflation target was 4.5% along with a tolerance band of 2.5% but actual inflation for the year was 6.87% which was within the tolerance band but above the midpoint target. From 2006 to 2016, inflation target was set at 4.5% along with a tolerance band of 2%. Actual inflation over these years fell within the tolerance band except for the years 2011, 2015 and 2016. In 2011, actual inflation was 6.64% which is slightly above the upper limit of the tolerance band. In 2015 and 2016, actual inflation stood at 9.03% and 8.74%, respectively, exceeding the upper limit of the inflation tolerance band set for these years. From 2017 to 2020, the target inflation rate was 4.5% along with a tolerance band of 1.5%. Actual inflation has consistently fallen within the tolerance band and indeed below the midpoint target. So, while inflation targets have been achieved in some years, clear breaches of the publicly announced inflation targets have also been recorded. Such mixed performances blot credibility building, especially for the purposes of guiding the inflation expectations of the public to the publicly communicated targets.

Chile

Chile's inflation performance pre-inflation targeting regime was better relative to Brazil, its South American counterpart. The country's inflation rate averaged 19.11% over the period 1978 and 1998. There were relatively inflationary periods though, especially in the 1970s and early parts of 1980s, with inflation peaking at 40.09% in 1978 over the review period. Following the adoption of inflation targeting in 1999, inflation rates plummeted, reaching a minimum of 0.35% in 2009 and an average of 3.17% over the inflation targeting period. Inflation did rise occasionally, with a peak of 8.72% in 2008, but was far below the pre-inflation targeting levels (See Table 2.2 and Figure 2.2). Interestingly, however, the inflation targeting regime exhibited greater variability in inflation rates relative to the prior period. The coefficient of variation of

Table 2.2 Descriptive statistics on inflation rate in Chile

	Before Inflation Targeting	*Inflation Targeting Period*
Mean	19.11	3.17
Maximum	40.09	8.72
Minimum	5.11	0.35
Standard Deviation	10.00	1.69
Coefficient of Variation	0.52	0.53
Number of Observations	21	21

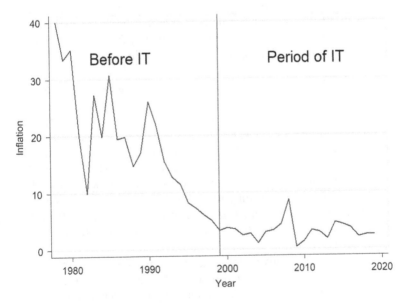

Figure 2.2 Inflation before and during IT in Chile.

the inflation rates during the inflation targeting period is marginally above that of the prior period, as per Table 2.2.

It stands to reason, therefore, that although inflation targeting regime witnessed lower inflation rates relative to the prior period, prices were less stable compared to the prior period. Meanwhile, price stability is an important ingredient in the inflation targeting framework proposition beyond achieving low prices.

Further, the achievement of low prices must be measured against the publicly announced inflation targets to make complete sense. Since the launch of full-fledged inflation targeting in 1999, actual inflation performance has been mixed, with inflation falling below the lower tolerance band in some periods and exceeding the upper tolerance band in others. In 2004, 2009, 2010 and 2013 for instance, inflation fell below the lower tolerance band of 2%, recording inflation rates of 1.055%, 0.35%, 1.41% and 1.79%, respectively. Meanwhile, inflation exceeded the upper tolerance band of 4% in 2007, 2008, 2014 and 2015 with respective inflation rates of 4.41%, 8.72%, 4.72% and 4.35%.

Colombia

Inflation in Colombia, prior to the adoption of inflation targeting regime in 1999, was consistently a double-digit phenomenon especially from the late 1970s, averaging 23.20% between 1978 and 1998 and peaking at 30.35% in 1991. Single-digit inflation became a reality only a year after the adoption of inflation targeting framework, with inflation rate of 9.22% in 2000. Inflation rate declined further under the inflation targeting regime (see Figure 2.3), reaching a minimum of 2.02% in 2013 and averaging 5.28% between 1999 and 2019 as given in Table 2.3.

Although low prices were achieved over the inflation targeting period, price levels were less stable under the inflation targeting framework compared to the prior period. The coefficient of variation in the observed inflation rates over the inflation targeting regime is 0.45, which is more than twice that of the prior period. This is far from ideal as prices are expected not only to be low but also stable. This is particularly problematic for inflation forecasting purposes and affects the inflation expectation formation of the public, which are critical success factors for the inflation targeting regime.

On whether the relatively low-price levels reflected the publicly announced inflation targets, it is observed that since the launch of the inflation targeting in 1999, inflation has largely breached not only the midpoint target of 3%, but has exceeded even the upper band of 4% of

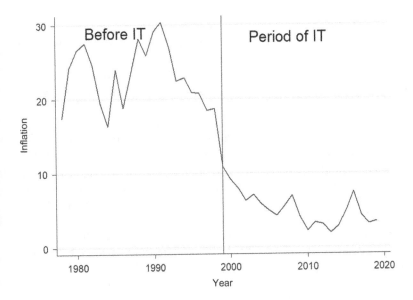

Figure 2.3 Inflation before and during IT in Colombia.

Table 2.3 Descriptive statistics on inflation rate in Colombia

	Before Inflation Targeting	*Inflation Targeting Period*
Mean	23.20	5.28
Maximum	30.35	10.87
Minimum	16.36	2.02
Standard Deviation	4.08	2.35
Coefficient of Variation	0.18	0.45
Number of Observations	21	21

the tolerance range. In the first year of the inflation targeting frame-work, actual inflation stood at 10.87%, more than twice the upper tolerance band. Although actual inflation declined marginally to 9.22% in the following year (2000), it was still more than twice the upper band of the inflation tolerance range. Actual inflation breached the upper tolerance band in the subsequent years up to 2009. Inflation only dropped to the tolerance band between 2010 and 2014. In 2015, 2016 and 2017, actual inflation breached the tolerance band once again but softened since 2018 to within the tolerance band.

Ghana

The early 1990s in Ghana were challenging for monetary policy authorities as inflation rates were worryingly high. Between 1994 and 1995, inflation rate was more than doubled, rising from 24.87% in 1994 to 59.46% in 1995. Although it dropped slightly to 46.56% in 1996, it was still close to twice the levels recorded in 1994. Between 1994 and 2006, inflation rate averaged 24.93%, with a minimum of 10.92% in 2006 and a maximum of 59.46% in 1995 (see Table 2.4).

Following the adoption of inflation targeting in 2007, inflation rates trended downwards, reaching a minimum of 7.13% in 2012 (see Figure 2.4) and an average of 12.48%. In terms of variability, the period of inflation targeting recorded a coefficient of variation of 0.34 compared to 0.58 for the prior period, implying a relative price stability in the inflation targeting era.

Comparing the relatively low and stable prices in the inflation targeting regime to the publicly announced targets reveals a worrying trend. The inflation outcome in Ghana, since the launch of the targeting framework in 2007, has been far from the announced targets. In 2007, the target range was 7%–9% and yet the actual inflation was 12.7%, breaching the upper band of the target. In 2008, actual inflation was 18.13% as against a target range of 6%–8%. The story is not different for 2009, 2013, 2014, 2015, 2016 and 2017. It was only in 2010, 2011 and 2012 that the central bank achieved the inflation target and a single digit for that matter.

Hungary

In spite of the double-digit inflation phenomenon between 1988 and 1998, Hungary's inflation footprint prior to the adoption of inflation targeting framework is relatively better than most, if not all, of the

Table 2.4 Descriptive statistics on inflation rate in Ghana

	Before Inflation Targeting	After Inflation Targeting
Mean	24.93	12.48
Maximum	59.46	19.25
Minimum	10.92	7.13
Standard Deviation	14.56	4.26
Coefficient of Variation	0.58	0.34
Number of Observations	13	13

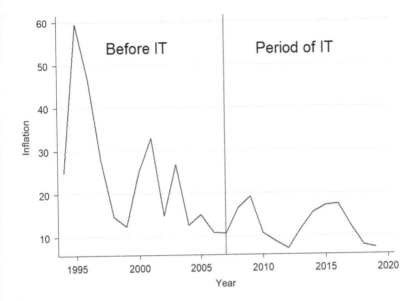

Figure 2.4 Inflation before and during IT in Ghana.

Table 2.5 Descriptive statistics on inflation rate in Hungary

	Before Inflation Targeting	After Inflation Targeting
Mean	16.24	4.02
Maximum	34.82	9.12
Minimum	5.29	−0.23
Standard Deviation	8.74	2.54
Coefficient of Variation	0.54	0.63
Number of Observations	19	19

emerging market countries under consideration. Between 1982 and 2000, inflation rate averaged 16.24% with a single-digit inflation rate in a number of years (from 1982 to 1987 and 1999 to 2000) prior to the inflation targeting adoption. The adoption of inflation targeting framework in 2001 engendered disinflation, with inflation rate averaging 4.02% over the inflation targeting era (see Table 2.5 and Figure 2.5).

Indeed, the highest inflation rate recorded under the inflation targeting regime (9.12%) in 2001 was still in the single-digit range.

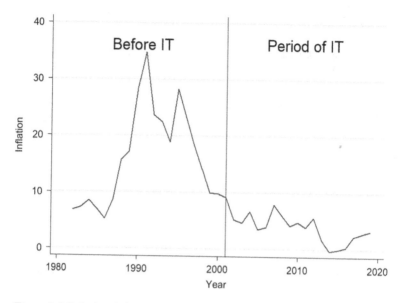

Figure 2.5 Inflation before and during IT in Hungary.

Although the inflation targeting period witnessed low price levels, it exhibited greater variability than the prior period. That is, the price levels were less stable in the inflation targeting period (with a coefficient of variation of 0.63) relative to the prior period (with 0.54 coefficient of variation).

Putting actual inflation side by side with the publicly announced inflation target shows mixed results. Inflation targeting framework was implemented in June 2001 with a target of 7% set for the year and 4.5% for the following year (2002). Actual inflation of 9.12% in 2001 and 5.27% in 2002 breached the respective targets for those years. Subsequently, targets of 3.5%, 3.5%, 4% and 3.5% were set for 2003, 2004, 2005 and 2006, respectively, with each of these targets determined two years prior to the reference year. Actual inflation in these years was respectively 4.66%, 6.74%, 3.56% and 3.93%, implying that the target was achieved only in 2005. A medium-term inflation target of 3% was set in August 2005 and remained so until March 2015 when a tolerance band of 1% was added to the 3%. From 2005 to 2015, the 3% medium-term target was achieved only in 2013, 2014 and 2015. From 2015 to 2019, the inflation rate has remained within the tolerance band of 2%–4%.

Indonesia

Inflation in Indonesia at the beginning of the 1990s was relatively benign, recording consistent single-digit rates from 1990 to 1997. By 1998, however, inflation had gone berserk, soaring to as high as 58.45% as the Asian financial crisis took a significant bite. Inflation dropped substantially to 20.48% in 1999 and further down to 3.69% in 2000. Inflationary momentum picked up in 2001, reaching 11.5% in that year and a further 11.9% in 2002. Following the adoption of inflation targeting in 2005, inflation averaged 6.14%, with a peak of 13.11% in 2006 and a minimum of 3.03% in 2019 (see Table 2.6).

Relatively, inflation performance post inflation targeting implementation has been better compared to the prior period. Price levels did not only trend downwards (see Figure 2.6), but have generally been more stable compared to the prior period. The coefficient of variation for inflation targeting period is 0.48 compared to the 1.08 recorded for the prior period.

As to whether the low and stable prices observed under the inflation targeting regime reflected the publicly announced targets, the results are mixed. In 2005 when inflation targeting was adopted, the target was 6% with a tolerance band of 1%, implying an upper tolerance band of 7%. Meanwhile, the actual inflation for that year was 10.45%, breaching the upper tolerance band. In 2006, the target was 8% with a tolerance band of 1% and yet actual inflation breached the target once again to reach 13.11%. In the following year (2007), the target was revised downwards to 6% with a tolerance band of 1%. Actual inflation, which stood at 6.41%, fell within the tolerance band. From 2008 to 2011, inflation targets were respectively 5%, 4.5%, 5% and 5% along with a 1% tolerance band. Actual inflation for these years was respectively 10.23%, 4.39%, 5.13% and 5.36%. Thus, whiles the targets were met in 2009, 2010 and 2011, the target for 2008 was breached. Between 2012 and 2014, the

Table 2.6 Descriptive statistics on inflation rate in Indonesia

	Before Inflation Targeting	Inflation Targeting Period
Mean	12.36	6.14
Maximum	58.45	13.11
Minimum	3.69	3.03
Standard Deviation	13.30	2.96
Coefficient of Variation	1.08	0.48
Number of Observations	15	15

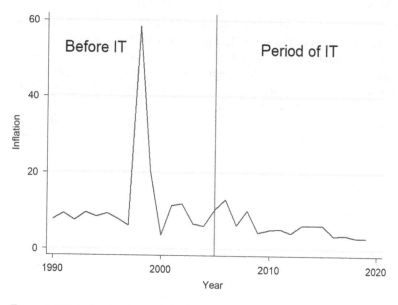

Figure 2.6 Inflation before and during IT in Indonesia.

target remained 4.5% along with a tolerance band of 1%. Save 2012 where actual inflation of 4.28% fell within the tolerance band, the announced target was breached in 2013 and 2014, with respective inflation rates of 6.41% and 6.39%. In 2015, the target was 4% with a tolerance band of 1% but actual inflation breached this target to close the year at 6.36%. The inflation target remained 4% along with 1% tolerance band in 2016 and 2017, with actual inflation rates of 3.53% and 3.81%, respectively, falling within the tolerance band. Similarly, the inflation target was 3.5% along with a tolerance band of 1% in 2018 and 2019, with actual inflation of 3.2% and 3.03%, respectively, falling within the inflation tolerance band.

Mexico

Mexico, arguably, is a classic case of how inflation targeting framework can engender disinflationary momentum. The country, prior to the adoption of inflation targeting framework, had witnessed an average inflation rate of 44.72% between 1982 and 2000. There were instances of inflation rates as high as 101.88% in 1983, 114.16% in 1988 and 131.83% in 1987. Following the adoption of inflation targeting framework in 2001, inflation rates dropped (see Figure 2.7) to an average of 4.33% between 2001 and 2019 (see Table 2.7). The minimum inflation rate observed in the prior period is more than the highest inflation rate recorded under the inflation targeting framework. Such is the phenomenal disinflationary momentum ignited by the adoption of inflation targeting framework in Mexico.

More importantly, the observed low prices were also more stable relative to the inflation rates observed in the prior regime. The coefficient of

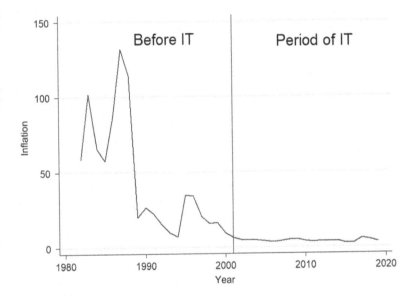

Figure 2.7 Inflation before and during IT in Mexico.

Table 2.7 Descriptive statistics on inflation rate in Mexico

	Before Inflation Targeting	*Inflation Targeting Period*
Mean	44.72	4.33
Maximum	131.83	6.37
Minimum	6.97	2.72
Standard Deviation	38.56	0.97
Coefficient of Variation	0.86	0.22
Number of Observations	19	19

variation for the inflation targeting period is 0.22 compared to the 0.86 recorded for the prior period.

In respect of the actual inflation versus the publicly announced target, Mexico has had mixed results, although actual inflation has fallen within the target range of 2%–4% (thus, 3% plus a tolerance band of 1%) on a number of occasions since the launch of the inflation targeting framework.

Russia

The pre-inflation targeting period in Russia was characterised by steep volatilities in price levels. Inflation in 1994 was a whopping 307.72% but fell sharply to 197.41% in 1995, 47.75% in 1996 and 14.76% in 1997. Inflationary momentum picked up briefly in 1998, reaching 27.69% and more than tripled to 85.75% in 1999. In 2000, inflation fell sharply to 20.8%, and by 2006, it had reached 9.67%. The inflation targeting period, on the other hand, has witnessed substantially low and stable price levels. Since the launch of the inflation targeting framework, inflation has averaged 7.95%, with a minimum of 2.88% in 2018 and a maximum of 15.53% in 2015 (see Table 2.8 and Figure 2.8).

The coefficient of variation for the inflation targeting period is 0.48 compared to 1.50 (three times) for the prior period, implying greater stability in prices during the inflation targeting period relative to the prior period.

Although inflation has trended downwards since the launch of inflation targeting framework in 2007, the levels observed post inflation targeting have remained above the announced annual inflation target of 4%. In 2007 when the inflation targeting framework was unveiled, actual inflation was 9.01%. Inflation increased further to 14.11% in 2008, declined to 11.65% in 2009 and reached 5.07% in 2012. By 2015,

Table 2.8 Descriptive statistics on inflation rate in Russia

	Before Inflation Targeting	After Inflation Targeting
Mean	60.47	7.95
Maximum	307.72	15.53
Minimum	9.67	2.88
Standard Deviation	90.58	3.85
Coefficient of Variation	1.50	0.48
Number of Observations	13	13

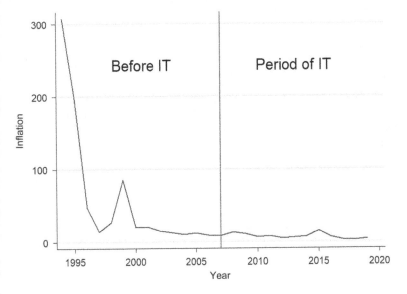

Figure 2.8 Inflation before and during IT in Russia.

however, inflation had taken an upward trajectory to reach 15.53, almost four times the inflation target. It was only in 2017 and 2018 that inflation fell below the announced target, recording 3.68% and 2.88%, respectively. In 2019, actual inflation breached the target once again, standing at 4.47%.

South Africa

South Africa's inflation rates between 1980 and 1999 averaged 12.24%, with a minimum of 5.18% in 1999 and a maximum of 18.65% in 1986, representing a far better performance than a number of the emerging market economies under consideration. With the launch of inflation targeting framework in the year 2000, inflation levels declined even further, averaging 5.3% over the period (see Table 2.9 and Figure 2.9).

However, the period before inflation targeting exhibited greater price stability relative to the inflation targeting period. Whereas the prior inflation targeting period recorded a coefficient of variation of 0.30, the inflation targeting period registered almost 50% more variability in prices, with a coefficient of variation of 0.44.

With inflation target range of 3%–6%, South Africa's inflation performance has been mixed. While actual inflation rates fell within the target

Table 2.9 Descriptive statistics on inflation rate in South Africa

	Before Inflation Targeting	After Inflation Targeting
Mean	12.24	5.30
Maximum	18.65	10.06
Minimum	5.18	−0.69
Standard Deviation	3.69	2.33
Coefficient of Variation	0.30	0.44
Number of Observations	20	20

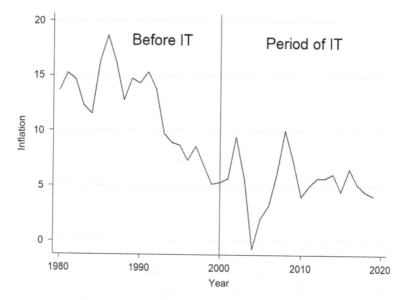

Figure 2.9 Inflation before and during IT in South Africa.

range in most of the years since the launch of the framework, the target was breached in 2002, 2007, 2008, 2009, 2014 and 2016, with respective inflation rates of 9.50%, 6.17%, 10.06%, 7.27%, 6.14% and 6.60%.

Turkey

Turkey's pre-inflation targeting period was not only inflationary, but also exhibited significant price volatilities over that period. In 1992, inflation rate was 70.08% but fell to 66.09% in the following year

(1993). Inflation rate almost doubled in 1994, reaching 105.22%. It slowed to 89.11% in 1995, 80.41% in 1996 and back up to 85.67% in 1997. By 2005, inflation had plummeted to 8.18%. On average, the inflation rate between 1992 and 2005 is 59.91% (see Table 2.10).

Following the implementation of inflation targeting framework, inflation has been relatively stable (see Figure 2.10), averaging 9.53% over the period and peaking at 16.33 in 2018. The disinflationary momentum had actually preceded the formal launch of the full-fledged inflation targeting framework in 2006, with inflation declining sharply

Table 2.10 Descriptive statistics on inflation rate in Turkey

	Before Inflation Targeting	After Inflation Targeting
Mean	59.91	9.53
Maximum	105.22	16.33
Minimum	8.18	6.25
Standard Deviation	30.16	2.97
Coefficient of Variation	0.50	0.31
Number of Observations	14	14

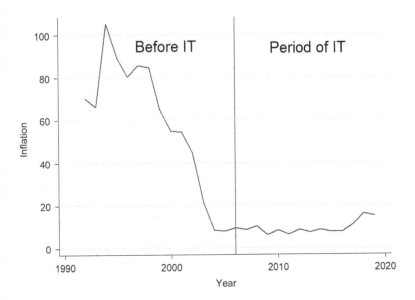

Figure 2.10 Inflation before and during IT in Turkey.

over the implicit targeting period (2002–2006). The relative stability of inflation over the inflation targeting period is evidenced by the lower coefficient of variation (0.31) compared to the prior period (0.5).

In 2002 when implicit inflation targeting started, actual inflation was 44.96% but declined sharply in 2003, recording 21.6%. By 2005 when implicit inflation targeting ended, actual inflation had dropped to 8.18%. Following the launch of formal inflation targeting in 2006, inflation ranged between 6.47% (recorded in 2011) and 16.33% (recorded in 2018). Since 2012 when the prevailing inflation target of 5% along with a tolerance band of 2% was set, inflation has consistently breached the upper tolerance band of 7%. In fact, inflation rates of 16.33% and 15.18% recorded in 2018 and 2019, respectively, were more than twice the upper limit of the tolerance band.

References

Alamsyah, H., Joseph, C., Agung, J., & Zulverdy, D. (2001). Towards implementation of inflation targeting in Indonesia. *Bulletin of Indonesian Economic Studies*, *37*(3), 309–324. https://www.bcb.gov.br/conteudo/home-en/FAQs/FAQ%2010-Inflation%20Targeting%20Regime%20in%20Brazil.pdf (Accessed on 14th July 2021).

Banco Central Do Brasil (2016). Inflation targeting regime in Brazil. Frequently asked question series. *A part of the financial education programme of the Central Bank of Brazil.*

Batini, N., & Laxton, D. (2007). Under what conditions can inflation targeting be adopted? The experience of emerging markets. *Series on Central Banking, Analysis, and Economic Policies*, (11).

Bawumia, M., Amoah, B., & Mumuni, Z. (2008). Choice of monetary policy regime in Ghana. *Bank of Ghana Working Paper*, WP/BOG-2008/07.

Carare, A., & Stone, R. (2003) Inflation targeting regimes. *IMF Working Paper*, WP/03/9.

Carrasco, C. A., & Ferreiro, J. (2013). Inflation targeting in Mexico. *Journal of Post Keynesian Economics*, *35*(3), 341–372.

Erdös, T. (2008). Inflation targeting in Hungary: A case study. *Acta Oeconomica*, *58*(1), 29–59.

Genc, I. H., & Balcilar, M. (2012). Effectiveness of inflation targeting in Turkey. *Emerging Markets Finance and Trade*, *48*(supp 5), 33–47.

Hamann, F., Hofstetter, M., & Urrutia, M. (2014). Inflation targeting in Colombia, 2002-12. *Economia*, *15*(1), 1–37.

Kenward, L. R. (2013). Inflation targeting in Indonesia, 1999–2012: An expost review. *Bulletin of Indonesian Economic Studies*, *49*(3), 305–327.

Libânio, G. (2010). A note on inflation targeting and economic growth in Brazil. *Brazilian Journal of Political Economy*, *30*(117), 73–88.

Masson, P. R., Savastano, M. A., & Sharma, S. (1997). The scope for inflation targeting in developing countries. *IMF Working Paper*, WP/97/130.

Mishkin, F. S. (2000). Inflation targeting in emerging market countries. *NBER Working Paper Series*, Working Paper 7618.

Morandé, F., & Schmidt-Hebbel, K. (2000). Monetary policy and inflation targeting in Chile. In *Inflation targeting in practice: Strategic and operational issues and application to emerging market economies*, edited by M. I. Blejer, A. Ize, A. M. Leone, & S. Werlang. Internation Monetary Fund.

Ramos-Francia, M., & Garcia, A. T. (2005). Reducing inflation through inflation targeting: The Mexican experience. *Banco de México Working Papers*, No. 2005-01.

Schaechter, A., Stone, M. R., & Zelmer, M. (2000). Adopting inflation targeting: Practical issues for emerging market countries. *IMF Occasional Paper* 202.

Svensson, L.E.O. (2011). Inflation targeting. In *Handbook of monetary economics*, edited by B. M. Friedman, & M. Woodford, Vol. 3B, Elsevier, pp. 1237–1302.

3 World food price paths, domestic food and overall prices and monetary policy conduct

Introduction

The challenges that food inflation poses to monetary policy authorities practicing inflation targeting are well acknowledged in the literature. The context of emerging and developing economies is even more dramatic, given the weight of food in the basket of household consumption in these economies. Understanding food price dynamics and the implications for monetary policy conduct is an invaluable adventure that is undertaken in this chapter. This chapter looks at the world food price movements and the food price dynamics in the selected countries being studied. It then relates food prices to the paths of overall prices in these countries. The implications for monetary policy are discussed. Given that the chapter is largely descriptive in nature, using monthly or quarterly data would mean a consideration for a large amount of information even for a single year and that could make the chapter rather voluminous. For brevity, this chapter relies on annual data. For the world food prices, annual data are obtained from the Food and Agriculture Organisation (FAO) and start from 1991. To relate the dynamics of domestic food prices of the countries being studied to the global perspective, annual food inflation data for each of these countries are obtained from 1991 where data are available. For some countries such as Colombia, Ghana, Indonesia and Russia, data available start later than 1991. The annual food inflation data for Brazil, Chile, Hungary, Indonesia, Mexico, South Africa and Turkey are obtained from the Federal Reserve Economic Data (FRED) of St. Louis Federal Reserve Bank. Food inflation data on Colombia and Russia were also obtained from the FRED but were originally in quarterly series which were then averaged to obtain annual series. For Ghana, annual food inflation data were sourced from the economic time series database of the Bank of Ghana.

DOI: 10.4324/9781003195368-3

Developments in world food prices

The world food prices have been far from stable (see Figure 3.1) since the 1990s, with steep rises and declines over the period. Between 1990 and 1991, the global food price index declined by 1.51% on the back of major declines in the indices of sub-components such as sugar, cereals and meat. The sugar price index declined by 28.6% followed by a decline of 1.12% in the meat price index and 0.37% in the cereals price index. In 1992, the global food price index recovered from the previous year's decline to grow by 3%, driven by large increases in the indices of dairy, cereals and oils prices. Declines in the price indices of meat (4.44%), dairy (11.29%) and cereals (3.2%) in 1993 brought the overall global food prices down by 3.11% in that year. In 1994, the global food price index shot up by 8.1%, a recovery from the previous year's 3.11% decline. The sharp increase in the global food price index was occasioned by rises in the price indices of oils (33.2%), sugar (20.82%), cereals (4.94%) and meat (1.7%). The global food price index grew further by 14.47% in 1995 on the back hikes in the price indices of dairy (32.3%), meat (12.35%), cereals (14.39%), oils (11.27%) and sugar (9.68%). From a growth of 14.47% in 1995, global food price index grew by only 1.32% in 1996, plummeted by 9.1% in 1997 and

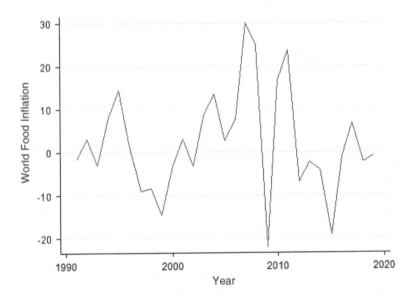

Figure 3.1 Trends in global food prices.

further down by 14.7% in 1999. The sharp decline in the global food price index in 1999 was driven by declines in indices such as sugar (29.74%), oils (30.59%), cereals (9.82%), dairy (13.4%) and meat (6.1%). From a steep decline, global food prices rose sharply by 8% in 2003 and ballooned to a growth of 29.9% in 2007 when the global economic crisis started.

The dynamics of the global food price index between 2007 and 2011 was rather eventful, and unsurprisingly so, given the peculiarity of that period as the world witnessed an economic debacle on a spectacular scale. The period saw substantial swings in the global food price index, growing by as much as 29.9% and 24.7% in 2007 and 2008, respectively, plummeted substantially by 22% in 2009, grew by 16.5% in 2010 and further up by 23.55% in 2011. The steep increase in 2007 was driven by sharp increases in the price indices of dairy (67.55%), cereals (41.7%), oils (52.12%) and meat (8.99%). The growth of 24.7% in the global food price index in 2008 was fuelled by the increases in the price indices of cereals (36.4%), oils (31.44%) sugar (26.98%), meat (17.3%) and dairy (8.12%). In 2009, when the global food price index dropped steeply, it was on the back of sharp declines in the price indices of oils (33.1%), dairy (30.93%) and cereals (29.4%). When the global food price index resumed an upward trend in 2010, the growth in the price indices of oils (30.1%), dairy (22.42%), sugar (17.37%), meat (12.04%) and cereals (10.61%) played a significant role. The year 2011 was not different, with growth in the price indices of cereals (32.24%), oils (28.31%), sugar (22.15%), dairy (16.1%) and meat (15.76%) fuelling the overall 23.55% increase in the global food price index. From 2012 to 2019, the global food price index largely declined, with positive growth recorded only in 2017 (6.63%).

Food inflation dynamics in domestic economies

The trajectory of the world food prices has been one of instabilities. Whether the food inflation paths in the countries under study exhibited the swings observed on the global scale is an important consideration for this section. Except the early 1990s, Brazil's food inflation has been relatively stable, especially after 1995 (see Figure 3.2). From a three-digit food inflation rate in 1991, Brazil's food inflation reached a four-digit zone in 1992, recording 1090.6%. Food inflation rate almost doubled in 1993, reaching 1949.8% and peaking at 2280.13% in 1994.

In 1995, food inflation in Brazil dropped sharply to the double-digit range, recording 58.5%. The disinflationary momentum continued in 1996, with food inflation dropping to a single-digit rate of 5.92% and

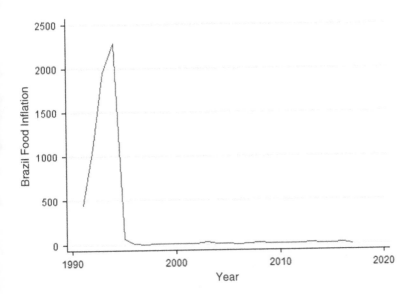

Figure 3.2 Food prices in Brazil.

remained in the single-digit range until 2003 when it shot up to 20.36%. It declined sharply to 4% in 2004 and further down to 3.1% and 0.02% in 2005 and 2006, respectively. Between 2007 and 2011, when the global food prices saw major swings, food prices in Brazil mimicked a similar pattern. It jumped from 0.02% in 2006 to 6.78% in 2007, almost doubled to 13.1% in 2008, dropped sharply to 5.79% in 2009, increased to 6.1% in 2010 and further up to 8.85% in 2011. Food inflation dropped marginally to 8.14% in 2012, increased to 11.21% in 2013, fell to 7.55% in 2014, increased to 9.8% in 2015 and further up to 11.54% in 2016.

Chile's food prices since the 1990s have been characterised by steep declines and rises (see Figure 3.3). From 25.82% in 1991, food prices dropped to 17.96% in 1992, 10.87% in 1993 and by 1999, it had reached negative 0.19%. It began to rise steadily from the year 2000, reaching 3.26% in 2003, dropped sharply to negative 1.92% in 2004, rose again to 2.87% in 2005 and slowed marginally to 2.6% in 2006.

In 2007, food prices in Chile almost quadrupled, increasing from 2.6% in 2006 to 9.6% and peaked at 17.18% in 2008. In 2009, food prices declined sharply to 4.38%, further down to 2.2% in 2010 and tripled to 6.7% in 2011. It increased marginally to 7.62% in 2012, dropped to 4.39% in 2013, increased to 6.97% and 7.11% in 2014 and

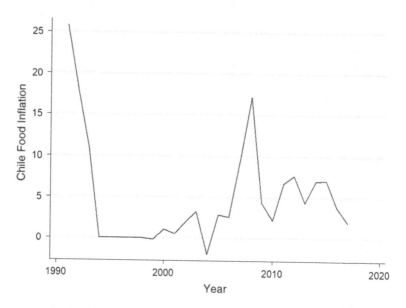

Figure 3.3 Food prices in Chile.

2015, respectively, dropped sharply to 3.82% in 2016 and further down to 2% in 2017.

Food inflation in Colombia witnessed similar unstable patterns over the years (see Figure 3.4). Food inflation dropped marginally from 15.93% in 1996 to 15.71% in 1997, increased to 22.64% in 1998 and dropped sharply to 6.51% in 1999. It shot up to 9.56% in 2000 and remained relatively stable up to 2003 when food inflation stood at 8.13%. It then declined to 6.36% and 6.37% in 2004 and 2005, respectively, and dropped to 5.58% in 2006.

In 2007, food inflation shot up to 8.42%, increasing further to 12.38% in 2008. It then dropped sharply to 3.72% and 0.22% in 2009 and 2010, respectively. In 2011, it increased significantly to 4.57%, declined to 3.43% and 0.42% in 2012 and 2013, respectively, and increased to 2.97% in 2014. In 2015, food prices almost quadrupled to reach 8.62% and further up to 13.19% in 2016. Food inflation then dropped steeply to below 1% in 2017 and 2018.

Ghana's food inflation path has had its own unstable characteristics (see Figure 3.5), increasing from 7.53% in 2006 to 10.51% in 2007 and further up to 16.73% in 2008. It then declined to 11.85% in 2009 and steeply down to 6.39% in 2010.

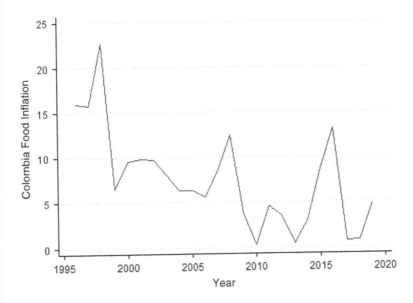

Figure 3.4 Food prices in Colombia.

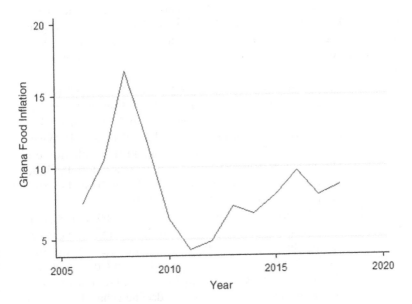

Figure 3.5 Food prices in Ghana.

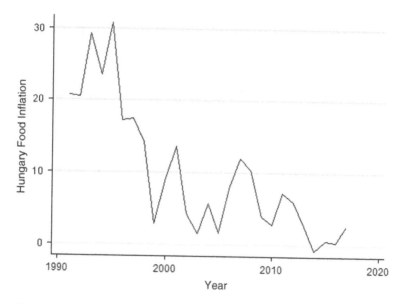

Figure 3.6 Food prices in Hungary.

In 2011, food inflation declined further to 4.27%, increased marginally to 4.85% in 2012 and further up to 7.24% in 2013. Food prices declined marginally to 6.76% in 2014 and increased to 8% and 9.69% in 2015 and 2016, respectively. It declined to 8% in 2017 but rose to 8.69% in 2018.

In Hungary, food price inflation has been relatively high and unstable since the 1990s (see Figure 3.6). Food inflation increased from 20.55% in 1992 to 29.31% in 1993. It declined to 23.55% in 1994 but rose to peak at 30.81% in 1995. There was a sharp decline in 1996 when food inflation reached 17.3%. A steady decline in food inflation continued in the subsequent years, reaching 1.66% in 2005. Food inflation picked up thereafter, increasing sharply to 8.17% in 2006, 11.94% in 2007 and dropping marginally to 10.39% in 2008.

Food inflation dropped to 3.89% and 2.78% in 2009 and 2010, respectively, but rose to 7.24% in 2011. Since 2012, food inflation has been on the decline, reaching a negative 0.80% in 2014 and 2.63% by 2017.

Indonesia's food inflation over the period exhibited considerable swings (see Figure 3.7), increasing from 8.66% in 1997 to a whooping 92.56% in the following year (1998). It then declined sharply to 25% in 1999 and further down to negative 4.78% in the year 2000. Food

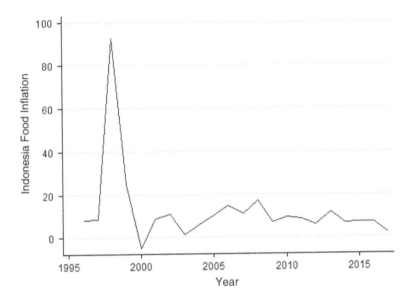

Figure 3.7 Food prices in Indonesia.

inflation then rose to 8.43% and 10.83% in 2001 and 2002, respectively, but declined sharply to 1.1% in 2003.

In 2004, food inflation rose to 5.9%, reaching a double-digit range from 2005 up to 2008. In 2005, food inflation in Indonesia almost doubled to 10.3% and further up to 14.85% in 2006. It declined to 10.95% in 2007 but rose to 16.96% in 2008. By 2012, it had declined to 5.86% but almost doubled in 2013 as food inflation stood at 11.82%. In 2014, it dropped to 6.82% but rose marginally to 7.17% and 7.24% in 2015 and 2016, respectively.

Food inflation in Mexico, especially in the 1990s, was considerably unstable (see Figure 3.8). From 19.31% in 1991, food inflation declined steadily to 4.65% in 1994 but rose steeply to 39.63% and 42.25% in 1995 and 1996, respectively. Although it dropped sharply to 19.11% in 1997, it remained within the double-digit range up to 1999.

Food inflation declined sharply to 5.42% in 2000 and remained within the single-digit range. There were intermittent increases in food inflation in 2004, 2008, 2009 and 2012, but they were all within the single-digit range.

Russia's food inflation rates have been relatively low since 2005 but not without swings (see Figure 3.9). Food inflation rates ranged

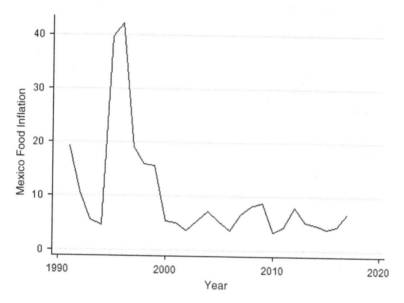

Figure 3.8 Food prices in Mexico.

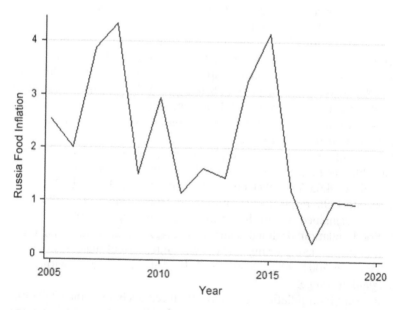

Figure 3.9 Food prices in Russia.

between 0.22% in 2017 and 4.35% in 2008. In 2005, food inflation was 2.53%, dropped to 1.99% in 2006 but rose to 3.87% and 4.35% in 2007 and 2008, respectively.

Food inflation dropped thereafter to 1.5% in 2009, almost doubled to 2.94% in 2010, declined by more than half to reach 1.14% in 2011 and remained relatively stable until 2013. In 2014, it shot up to 3.26% and reached 4.17% in 2015. Food inflation has since declined consistently, reaching 0.96% in 2019.

The early 1990s saw high food inflation levels in South Africa (see Figure 3.10), with food inflation increasing from 19.64% in 1991 to 25.25% in 1992. It dropped sharply to 6.8% in 1993 but rose to 13.76% in 1994. Food inflation declined to 8.74% in 1995 and further down to 6.1% in 1996. It increased to 9.46% in 1997, declined to 6.16% and 4.89% in 1998 and 1999, respectively. In the year 2000, food inflation rose to 7.82%, dropped to 5.38% in 2001 and more than tripled to 17.39% in 2002.

Food inflation halved in 2003, reaching 8.16% and declined sharply to 1.42% in 2004. It inched up to 1.69% in 2005, increased consistently up to 2008 with food inflation rates of 5.96%, 10% and 15.5% in 2006, 2007 and 2008, respectively. Food inflation dropped to 9.34% in 2009

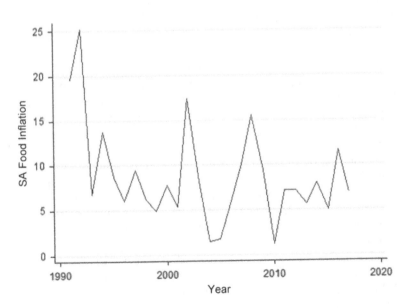

Figure 3.10 Food prices in South Africa.

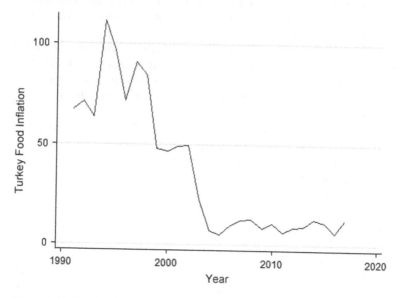

Figure 3.11 Food prices in Turkey.

and further downwards to 1.21%. It rose again to 7.1% and 7.2% in 2011 and 2012 respectively. In 2013, food inflation fell to 5.65%, rose to 8% in 2014, declined to 4.95% in 2015 but more than doubled to 11.66% in 2016.

Turkey's food inflation in the early 1990s, similar to Brazil, has been very high, recording a three-digit food inflation rate in the process (see Figure 3.11). Indeed, food inflation in Turkey, unlike Brazil, remained relatively high through the 1990s up to the early 2000s. Food inflation increased from 67.11% in 1991 to 71.34% in 1992, dropped to 63.51% in 1993 and ballooned to 111.87% in 1994.

Although food inflation declined thereafter, it remained very high and within the double-digit range. In 1995, food inflation dropped to 96.8%, then further down to 71.61% in 1996 but rose again to 90.92% in 1997. In 1998, it dropped to 84.48% and consistently thereafter until 2005 when it recorded 4.93%. It picked up in 2006, recording 9.70% and further up to 12.42% and 12.79% in 2007 and 2008, respectively. Food inflation slowed in 2009 to 8.02%, rose to 10.58% in 2010, dropped again to 6.24% in 2011 but rose again to reach 12.62% in 2014. Although it declined to 5.79% by 2016, it picked up to reach 12.7% in 2017.

From the foregoing, food prices, either at the global level or within the selected countries, have exhibited substantial swings over the period under review. Such swings are not healthy for the purpose of inflation forecasting which is critical for inflation targeting countries. This is particularly so in view of the large proportion of food in the basket of items used for the determination of consumer prices in these countries. This then creates the tendency for overall inflation to exhibit similar paths of instability and becomes a challenge for monetary policy authorities in forecasting and managing inflation within set targets.

Food prices and overall inflation

The sheer size of food in the emerging markets and developing economies' consumption baskets has prompted the assertion in the literature that the overall inflation paths in these economies are influenced, to a greater extent, by food price movements (see Iddrisu & Alagidede, 2020 and 2021 for detailed literature on this). In this respect, the current section looks at the paths of food and overall inflation in the selected emerging and developing countries.

Brazil

Food and overall inflation in Brazil have moved in unison over the period under review and have been virtually neck-to-neck (see Figure 3.12). Rises and falls in overall inflation are almost exactly mirrored by the paths of food inflation. In 1999, when inflation targeting started, food inflation was 3.42% and the corresponding overall inflation was 4.86%. In 2000, food inflation rose to 5.14% and the overall inflation also increased to 7% in the same year. Food inflation rose up to 20.36% by 2003 and overall inflation also reached 14.72%. Food inflation dropped significantly in 2004 to 4% and overall inflation fell from 14.72% to 6.6%.

The trend has been the same thereafter with the paths of both food and overall inflation virtually entwined.

Chile

The overall and food inflation paths in Chile are very much similar, although with occasional drifts dissimilar to the case of Brazil. What is particularly unique about the case of Chile is the fact that substantial drops or rises in the overall inflation coincided with periods when food inflation had experienced even greater declines or increases (see Figure 3.13).

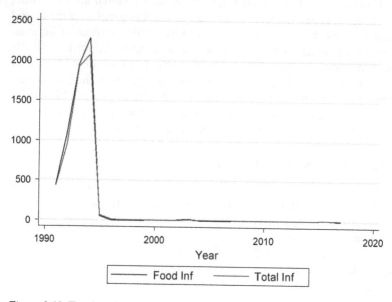

Figure 3.12 Food and overall inflation in Brazil.

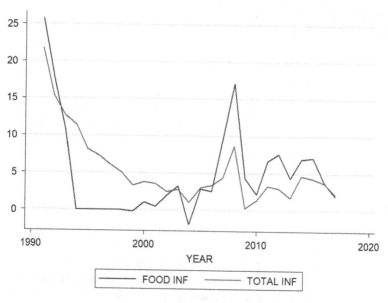

Figure 3.13 Food and overall inflation in Chile.

From Figure 3.13, steep falls in overall inflation saw food inflation below it and steep increases in overall inflation saw food inflation already above it. Such is the substantial role of food inflation in many emerging markets and developing economies and not just Chile.

Colombia

The trajectories of food and overall inflation in Colombia have largely been similar over the years (see Figure 3.14), although some divergence occurred. For instance, food inflation dropped from 8.13% in 2003 to 6.4% in 2004 and overall inflation also fell from 7.13% to 5.9% over the same period. From that period up to 2006, food inflation remained relatively stable and overall inflation exhibited a similar pattern. In 2007, food inflation increased from 5.58% in the previous year to 8.4%, with overall inflation increasing from 4.3% to 5.55% over the same period.

Food inflation surged to 12.4% in 2008 and overall inflation reached 7% from 5.55% in the previous year. Food inflation took a downward turn between 2009 and 2010 and overall inflation exhibited a similar trend. These similar trends abound over the period under review.

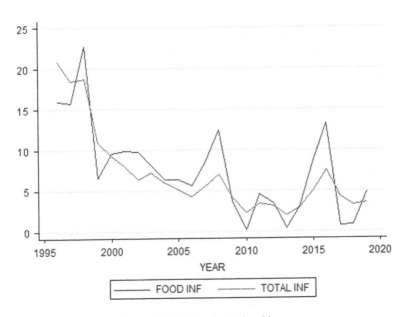

Figure 3.14 Food and overall inflation in Colombia.

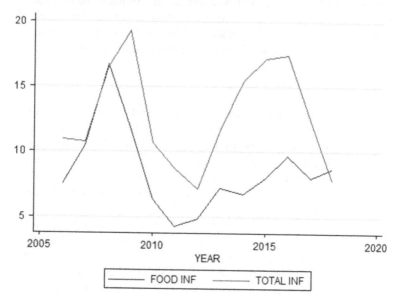

Figure 3.15 Food and overall inflation in Ghana.

Ghana

Ghana's inflation targeting was officially unveiled in 2007 when overall inflation stood at 10.73%. Food inflation in that year was 10.51%. Overall and food inflation in Ghana, similar to the other countries, have exhibited similar trends (see Figure 3.15). Food inflation shot up to 16.73% in 2008 and overall inflation reached 16.52%. Food inflation dropped to 11.85% in 2009 but overall inflation reached 19.3%.

By 2010, food inflation had dropped by almost half to 6.39% and overall inflation fell by almost half to 10.71%. In 2012, food inflation reached 4.85% and overall inflation dropped further to 7.13%. When food inflation took an upturn in 2013 to reach 7.24%, overall inflation increased to 11.67%. Indeed, the trends remained largely similar throughout the period under review.

Hungary

Similar to other countries, Hungary's food and overall inflation have also moved in unison over the period under review (see Figure 3.16). The falls and increases in food inflation closely mimicked the paths of the overall inflation in Hungary.

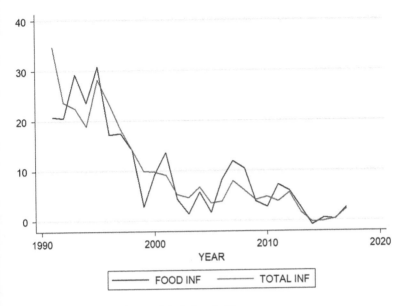

Figure 3.16 Food and overall inflation in Hungary.

Some drifts did occur over the period. For instance, when food inflation increased from 2.9% in 1999 to 9.2% in 2000, overall inflation declined marginally from approximately 10% to 9.8% over the same period. Largely, however, food and overall inflation moved together.

Indonesia

Similar to Chile, food inflation and overall inflation did not only move in a similar direction, but major increases or decreases in overall inflation saw food inflation already above or below it (see Figure 3.17).

In 1998, when food inflation increased steeply from 8.7% in the previous year to 92.56%, overall inflation increased from 6.23% to 58.45% over the same period. When food inflation dropped substantially to 25% in 1999, overall inflation dropped to 20.48%. Such similar trends are common over the sample period.

Mexico

Mexico's experience in respect of the paths of food and overall inflation is much akin to the case of Brazil (see Figure 3.18), with both food

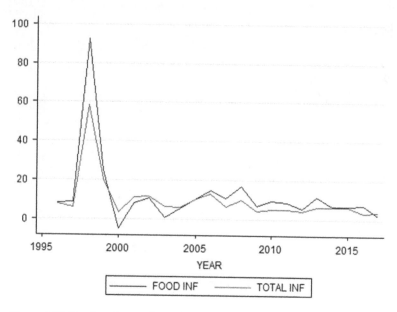

Figure 3.17 Food and overall inflation in Indonesia.

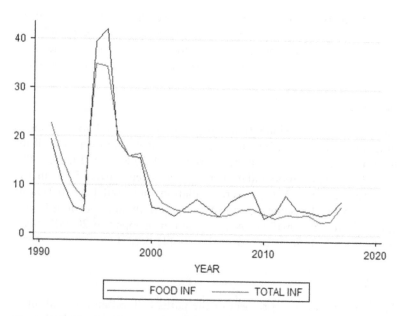

Figure 3.18 Food and overall inflation in Mexico.

and overall inflation series moving closely together. Between 1999 and 2000, food inflation dropped from 15.66% to 5.42% with overall inflation falling to 9.49% from 16.59% over the same period. Food inflation dropped further to reach 3.75% by 2002 and overall inflation also fell to 5.03%.

Over the sample period, as depicted in the figure above, overall and food inflation have fallen and risen in unison, highlighting the relevance of food inflation in the trajectory of overall inflation in Mexico.

Russia

Food and overall inflation in Russia have tended to move in the same direction over the period, although substantial gaps existed between the series over the period being studied (see Figure 3.19). Much as the series have had similar patterns, overall inflation tended to be higher than the food inflation series. In 2005, when food inflation was 2.53%, overall inflation was as high as 12.69%. Food inflation dropped to 1.99% in 2006 and the overall inflation also fell to 9.67% over the same period. By 2008, food inflation had risen to 4.35% and overall inflation reached 14.11%.

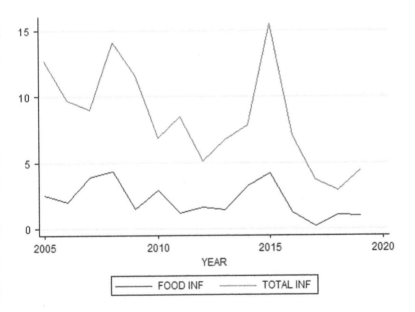

Figure 3.19 Food and overall inflation in Russia.

When food inflation dropped to 1.5% in the following year (2009), overall inflation also fell to 11.65%. Clearly, the two series have tended to move in unison but overall inflation remained higher than the levels of food inflation.

South Africa

South Africa's food and overall inflation story is not very different from the other countries observed earlier. Food and overall inflation paths have closely moved together over the period under review, although the direction of change in both series occasionally differed (see Figure 3.20).

Additionally, variations in food prices have been much substantial relative to overall inflation over the period under review. For instance, when food inflation dropped sharply from 25.3% in 1992 to 6.8% in 1993, overall inflation also dropped but from 13.9% to 9.72% over the same period. Similarly, when food inflation rose steeply in 2002 to reach 17.39% from 5.38% in the previous year, overall inflation also increased but from 5.7% to 9.5%.

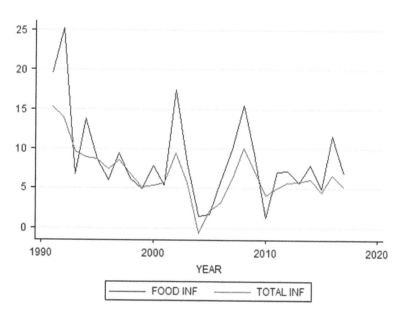

Figure 3.20 Food and overall inflation in South Africa.

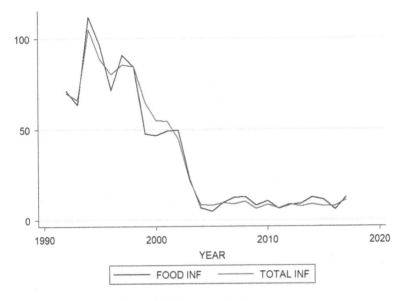

Figure 3.21 Food and overall inflation in Turkey.

Turkey

In Turkey, the paths of food and overall inflation have been very similar, akin to the case of Brazil. Food and overall inflation have moved together over the period (see Figure 3.21). Both food and overall inflation have been very high in the 1990s up to 2004 when they dropped in unison and remained below the previous levels since then.

Clearly, food and overall inflation in these countries have tended to move along similar paths and given the share of food in the consumption baskets of emerging and developing countries, food prices can play a major role in the trajectories of overall inflation that these countries target.

Food price persistence and volatility

Literature has widely asserted that food prices exhibit some persistence and volatilities (see Iddrisu & Alagidede, 2020 for a detailed exposition on this). The volatilities might not be surprising given the observed steep rises and falls in food prices observed in the earlier sections. In this regard, this section looks at the potential persistence and volatilities in food prices in the selected countries and what that means for overall inflation

Table 3.1 A gauge of food price persistence

	Coefficient	St. Errors	R-Squared	F-Statistics
Brazil	0.66***	0.15	0.43	18.22***
Chile	0.53***	0.12	0.47	20.88***
Colombia	0.46**	0.18	0.23	6.43**
Ghana	0.52*	0.27	0.28	3.8*
Hungary	0.79***	0.12	0.64	42.9***
Indonesia	0.11	0.23	0.01	0.24
Mexico	0.59***	0.16	0.36	13.21***
Russia	0.30	0.28	0.1	1.12
South Africa	0.26	0.18	0.08	2.08
Turkey	0.88***	0.09	0.80	89.22***

Note: *, ** and *** imply statistical significance at 10%, 5% and 1%, respectively. The coefficients are for the AR(1) of food inflation for the respective countries.

and monetary policy conduct. To gauge persistence, an autoregressive (AR) process is considered. A simple AR(1) is performed for the food price inflation of the respective countries. The results are presented in Table 3.1. A relatively high coefficient (close to 1) for the first lag of food inflation is an indication of food price persistence. For consistency in this chapter, the annual food inflation data used for the earlier subsections are maintained. It is important to point out that only Brazil, Chile, Hungary, Mexico, South Africa and Turkey have the same number of observations and could therefore be compared. Colombia, Ghana, Indonesia and Russia have varied observations, and therefore, their results are not comparable to each other nor the other six countries mentioned earlier.

For Russia, Indonesia and South Africa, the coefficients of the first lag of food inflation are below 1 but statistically insignificant. Countries such as Turkey, Hungary, Brazil, Chile, Ghana and Colombia have various degrees of food price persistence as per the statistically significant coefficients of the first lag of food inflation for these countries. Turkey has the relatively greatest food price persistence, followed by Hungary, Brazil, Mexico and Chile, respectively.

To gauge volatilities in the food prices of the various countries, the coefficient of variation is used. The results are presented in Table 3.2. Food price volatility in Brazil is substantial. Over the period under review, food prices in Brazil ranged from a minimum of 0.02% in 2006 to a maximum of 2280.13% in 1994 and a standard deviation as high as

Table 3.2 Food price volatility

	Mean	Maximum	Minimum	St. Deviation	C. of Variation
Brazil	221.48	2280.13	0.02	590.73	2.67
Chile	5.07	25.82	−1.93	6.50	1.28
Colombia	7.53	22.64	0.22	5.55	0.74
Ghana	7.89	16.73	0.00	3.86	0.49
Hungary	9.94	30.81	−0.80	9.05	0.91
Indonesia	12.49	92.56	−4.78	18.80	1.51
Mexico	10.13	42.25	3.31	10.00	0.99
Russia	2.15	4.35	0.22	1.30	0.61
South Africa	8.74	25.25	1.21	5.53	0.63
Turkey	37.20	111.87	4.93	33.87	0.91

Note: C. of variation means coefficient of variation. St. Deviation means standard deviation.

590.73. Unsurprisingly, the coefficient of variation is very high (2.67) indicating high volatility in food prices in the country.

Indonesia's food inflation is another that has exhibited substantial swings over the period for which data are available for the country. Food inflation ranged from −4.78% in 2000 to 92.56% in 1998. The standard deviation is 18.80 and an accompanying coefficient of variation of 1.51. Chile also witnessed one of the relatively volatile food price paths amongst the countries under study. Food prices in that country fell to a minimum of −1.93% in 2004 and peaked at 25.82% in 1991. The associated standard deviation is 6.50, and the coefficient of variation of 1.28. Other countries to have experienced relatively high volatility in food prices include Mexico, Hungary, Turkey and Colombia.

Implications of food price volatility and persistence for the conduct of monetary policy

Given the entwined paths of food and overall inflation, the observed volatilities in food prices pose a challenge to the conduct of monetary policy especially for central banks that target inflation. This is because the overall inflation trajectory would undoubtedly carry the features of food prices given the dominance of the latter in the determination of the former in many of these emerging markets and developing countries. Meanwhile, inflation forecasting is an important cornerstone for a successful inflation-targeting framework. Monetary policy authorities require a reasonably accurate forecast of the inflation path to be able to make appropriate policy decisions to guide inflation to the announced target. When future inflation is not amenable to accurate forecasts, determining the extent of policy tightening or easing would be problematic and achievement of the publicly announced inflation target is put in inevitable jeopardy. Meanwhile, missing the publicly announced inflation target dents the monetary authorities' credibility and affects their ability to guide the expectations of the public towards the inflation target.

The level of persistence in food prices is not helpful either. Such persistence implies that food prices are not likely to revert to the mean following a shock. Meanwhile, the food supply is one that is substantially susceptible to extreme shocks such as weather conditions. In such extreme shocks, food prices tend to surge and with the observed persistence, it leaves a prolonged upward bias in the path of overall inflation in these countries. One of the consequences is that overall inflation may breach the publicly announced inflation targets in the process. Unsurprisingly, many of these countries have missed the publicly announced inflation targets on some occasions over the inflation targeting periods. Another consequence is the fact that monetary policy authorities may be forced to take restrictive stands over a prolonged period and that could be deleterious for the growth prospects of these countries.

References

Iddrisu, A. A., & Alagidede, I. P. (2020). Monetary policy and food inflation in South Africa: A quantile regression analysis. *Food Policy*, 101816.

Iddrisu, A. A., & Alagidede, I. P. (2021). Asymmetry in food price responses to monetary policy: A quantile regression approach. *SN Business and Economics*, *1*, 52.

4 Monetary policy and food price inflation: A wavelet-based quantile regression analysis

Introduction

With the benefit of the understanding of the features of food prices, their role in overall inflation trajectory and the challenges that confront monetary policy authorities, an obvious question is whether monetary policy is capable of subduing food price inflation. The answer to this question is an empirical one which is dealt with in this chapter. This chapter lays out the theoretical and empirical literature and the associated gaps. It also presents the methodology and the findings of the study. Policy implications of these findings are discussed.

Theoretical and empirical literature

The theoretical literature on monetary policy-food inflation nexus has largely been focused on whether monetary policymakers should include food and other commodities such as oil in the measure of inflation for the purposes of targeting and welfare dynamics. The debate in the theoretical literature has been centred on the appropriate measure of inflation for the purposes of targeting by monetary policy authorities in a manner that exacts optimality in monetary policy conduct and economic welfare. Earlier proposition by Aoki (2001) is to the effect that central banks would deliver optimal monetary policy by targeting an inflation measure that excludes energy and food prices. The author argues that supply shocks have usually been gauged by changes in energy and food prices and because such changes are transient, central banks should exclude them from overall inflation measures. In a theoretical model, the author shows that the stabilisation of core inflation delivers a superior outcome than an inflation measure that includes energy and food prices.

However, Anand & Prasad (2010) and Anand et al. (2015) argued that the strength of the core inflation proposition is premised on the

DOI: 10.4324/9781003195368-4

presumption of complete financial markets. Meanwhile, households are confronted with financial frictions, especially in developing and emerging economies, which is a manifestation of incompleteness of financial markets. Frankel (2008) posited that the fact that agricultural goods exhibit volatility is not suggestive that they do not contain important information and neither is their exclusion from inflation measure for monetary policy purposes necessarily justifiable. Following the argument by Walsh (2011) that the core inflation proposition is premised on the assumption that core inflation is not impacted by non-core inflation in the long run, De Gregorio (2012) reckons that such an assumption has no basis in theory nor empirics. The author (De Gregorio, 2012) argues that because food dominates the consumption baskets of several emerging market countries, food prices can underpin pressures on wages and general price levels. Šoškić (2015) argues that the attempt to relate food price changes to supply side factors alone may not tell the entire story as hikes in food prices could also be demand-driven, underpinned by increases in household income. Gómez et al. (2012) reckoned that inflation targeting central banks of developing economies do not have the latitude to ignore prices of food in the measure of inflation they target, given the proportion of household income that food alone takes. Alper et al. (2016) argued that the sheer size of food in the consumption baskets of low-income countries makes core inflation an unrepresentative measure of living costs confronting households in these countries.

The backlash on the core inflation proposition by Aoki (2001) led to a number of other theoretical expositions. Anand & Prasad (2010, 2015) built a theoretical model that took financial constraints and frictions into consideration to determine the optimal consumer price index (CPI) that monetary policy authorities can target. Importantly, they incorporated emerging market characteristics, especially relating to food dominance in consumption baskets. They show that where financial constraints and frictions are present, core inflation targeting by monetary policy authorities deliver sub-optimal outcomes. Importantly, households are not sensitive to interest rates when they do not have access to financial markets.

In another theoretical study, Catao & Chang (2015) rather compared the optimality of targeting CPI or producer price index (PPI). They find that following a shock to global prices of food, targeting CPI delivers a welfare-enhancing outcome than the PPI. This is under the condition that there is a perfect sharing of international risk and the elasticity of the country's export prices is not very small. They posit that the welfare benefits are even more prominent when expected CPI (as opposed to just CPI) is targeted. They find further that the targeting of PPI only becomes superior under the condition that the sharing of international risk is incomplete.

Pourroy et al. (2016), in a theoretical model, studied the response of monetary policy to shocks from world prices of food. They find that monetary policy optimality is a function of the level of income of countries. Specifically, they find that monetary policy is optimal for medium and low-income countries when the policymakers target headline inflation in view of the dominance of food in the consumption basket of these countries as well as the composition of the food basket itself (a large share of goods that are not tradable). For high-income countries, they find that monetary policy optimality is exacted by targeting non-food inflation.

Ginn & Pourroy (2020) expanded the theoretical debate on the optimality of monetary policy that targets headline or core inflation by considering whether an intervention by fiscal authorities in a country where households are confronted with financial constraints affects the choice or outcome of core or headline inflation targeting. They did so by incorporating food price subsidy dimensions into the theoretical model. They show that where food price subsidy exists (intervention by fiscal authorities) and financial friction is present, a central bank delivers superior welfare by targeting headline inflation that embodies subsidies.

As observed by Bhattacharya & Jain (2020), authors who found monetary policy to engender stability in the prices of commodities such as Scrimgeour (2014), Akram (2009) and Frankel (2008) established three main channels for this effect. The first is that when monetary policy is restrictive, the cost of storage becomes prohibitive, occasioning stock depletion and increasing the supply of these commodities. The second channel works such that a monetary policy rate hike makes interest-bearing assets such as treasury bills attractive and therefore speculators adjust their investment portfolios by reducing holdings of commodities and in turn hold interest-bearing assets. The third channel, emphasised by Scrimgeour (2014), relates to the channel of aggregate demand (Bhattacharya & Jain, 2020).

Monetary policy, theoretically, can reduce food inflation through the moderation of aggregate demand in the economy (Bhattacharya & Jain, 2020). On the basis of the Engel's law, however, the effect of a restrictive monetary policy on non-food inflation would be greater than the effect on food inflation. In addition, the effect of a restrictive monetary policy on consumption of food could be significantly less in countries where food dominates the consumption basket and particularly when the majority of the population live and consume food at the level of subsistence. Such a restrictive policy would then have its impact felt on the prices of non-food instead. As a result, the consumption pattern and the developmental stage essentially inform the extent of restrictive policy impact (Bhattacharya & Jain, 2020). Invariably, therefore, if monetary policy responds in the wake of rising food prices, the combined effect on the non-food prices and to some extent the food prices would then have an impact on the overall inflation.

Although theoretical propositions differ in respect of whether core or headline inflation must be targeted when food inflation fuels general inflation, there is unanimity on the fact that when monetary policy is optimal, it helps to stabilise food inflation (Bhattacharya & Jain, 2020). As a consequence, empirical literature exploring the impact of monetary policy on food inflation is growing. Using a structural vector autoregressive model in the context of the United States, Akram (2009) finds a significant rise in prices of commodities when real interest rates decline. The author finds that the response of food prices in particular to the decline in real interest rates is gradual. Food prices respond positively to interest rate hikes initially, especially in the first one to two quarters but decline significantly thereafter. Anzuini et al. (2010) estimated the monetary policy impact on commodity prices. They find that the index of commodity prices rose in reaction to an accommodative monetary policy stance. Scrimgeour (2014) considered the impact on commodity prices when monetary policy changes. The author finds that when monetary policy changes, there is an immediate impact on the prices of commodities. Studying the United States context, Hammoudeh et al. (2015) used data in quarterly frequency from quarter one of 1957 to quarter three of 2008. The authors studied the monetary policy impact on the index of commodity prices (aggregate level) as well as the prices of the individual components including food (disaggregated level). They find that when monetary policy is restrictive in the United States, the effect on the total prices of commodities is negative and significant, although such an effect occurs with lags. On the disaggregated front, they find that an increase in the monetary policy rate impacts food inflation positively and the impact is persistent.

Wagan et al. (2018) studied monetary policy effect on food prices and growth of agriculture in Pakistan and India. Although the overall finding is that although food prices are reduced by monetary policy tightening, their results show that food prices in India respond positively to monetary policy during the initial three months as well as between the seventh and the nineth month. For Pakistan, a shock to monetary policy sees food prices rise between the second and the fourth months. Using quarterly data from quarter one of 2006 to quarter two of 2016, Bhattacharya & Jain (2020) studied how effective monetary policy is in providing stability in the prices of food. The authors considered a set of developed and emerging countries. The finding is that food inflation is positively impacted by a restrictive monetary policy that is unexpected for both emerging and developed countries. Specifically, the authors observed that when inflation momentum in the country is underpinned by food inflation, then a restrictive monetary policy destabilises both the food and general inflation. Iddrisu & Alagidede (2020) and (2021), respectively, studied the contexts of South Africa and Ghana. Both studies found monetary policy to impact food prices positively in South Africa and Ghana.

However, as indicated earlier, all these studies have been conducted in purely time domain. Meanwhile, economic processes and the resulting data that underlie these studies are necessarily an embodiment of different objectives of distinct economic agents that occur across varied horizons. This study breaks grounds in this strand of the literature by deploying wavelet-based quantile regression for the first time. Using wavelet, the series is decomposed into scales that reflect the different horizons inherent in economic processes and objectives of economic agents. The application of quantile regression aids in capturing outliers in food prices that thwart forecasting accuracy and also helps to capture asymmetry in the relationship between monetary policy and food prices.

Methodology

Data and sources

The data used is in monthly frequency starting from January 2006 to May 2018 for each of the ten countries being studied. Data availability for some of the countries informed the start and end of the data used for this study. Obviously, some of the countries have data prior to 2006 and after May 2018. However, for a meaningful comparison of the empirical results of the ten countries, it is prudent to use the same sample size for all the countries. Data were obtained on variables such as food inflation, monetary policy, real gross domestic product, real household consumption expenditure, real gross fixed capital formation, exchange rate of the respective countries' currencies against the United States dollar and world food price index. For Brazil, Chile, Colombia, Hungary, Indonesia, Mexico and Russia, data on monetary policy rate, real gross domestic product, real household consumption expenditure, real gross fixed capital formation and exchange rate of the respective countries' currencies against the United States dollar were obtained from the IMF's International Financial Statistics (IFS). The food inflation rate for these countries was obtained from the FRED database. It is important to mention that the data on real gross domestic product, real household consumption expenditure and real gross fixed capital formation were originally in nominal values but were deflated with the GDP deflator from the same source. Additionally, these series (real gross domestic product, real household consumption expenditure and real gross fixed capital formation) were initially in quarterly series but converted to monthly frequency.

For Ghana, the exchange rate and monetary policy rate data were taken from the IMF's IFS. Food inflation data were taken from the Bank of Ghana's website. Meanwhile, data on the real gross domestic product, real household consumption expenditure and real gross fixed capital formation were obtained from the Ghana Statistical Service and the World Development Indicators which were in annual frequency originally but converted to monthly frequency. For South Africa, the monetary policy rate (repo) and the exchange rate of the Rand to the dollar were taken from the IMF's IFS. Food inflation data were taken from the FRED database. Data on real gross domestic product, real household consumption expenditure and real gross fixed capital formation were obtained from the South African Reserve Bank and Statistics South Africa. For Turkey, food inflation data werer obtained from the FRED database and the monetary policy rate and the exchange rate data were obtained from the IMF's IFS. Meanwhile, data on the real gross domestic product, real household consumption expenditure and real gross fixed capital formation were obtained from the Turkish Statistical Institute. Data on world food prices (included in each country's model) were obtained from the United Nation's Food and Agriculture Organisation (FAO).

Definition of variables

Monetary policy rate (MPR) is the policy rate set by the central banks of the respective countries. It is expressed in percentage as determined by these central banks.

Food inflation (FOOD) is expressed in percentage and is measured as the change in the food CPI in a particular month from the same month in the previous year.

Real gross domestic product (RGDP) represents real output in the respective countries.

Household consumption expenditure (HCE) represents consumption expenditure (real) in the respective countries.

Gross fixed capital formation (GFCF) captures investment expenditure (real) in the respective countries.

Exchange rate (USD) represents the exchange rate of the respective countries' domestic currencies against the United States dollar.

Global food price index (GFPI) is expressed in percentage and represents the percentage change in the world food prices in a particular month from the same month in the previous year.

The estimation approaches

The wavelet analysis

Aguiar-Conraria et al. (2008) observed that although spectral analysis has enjoyed considerable usage in the economics literature to uncover relationships between various macroeconomic variables across different frequencies, apparent limitations include the loss of time information, the struggle by users to differentiate relationships that are ephemeral and the difficulty in the identification of structural breaks inherent in the series. In addition, the technique is suitable only in the cases of time series that possess properties known to be statistically stable. In other words, the technique is only applicable to time series data that are stationary. Meanwhile, economic time series are seldom stationary, exhibit complexity and fraught with considerable noise. The Fourier transform ameliorated these limitations as it disintegrates the initial time series into sub samples and then implement the Fourier transform on the respective sub samples. Such a process in a Fourier transform, however, suffers substantial inefficiencies and maintains a homogenous frequency resolution across various frequencies, a limitation that ushered in the wavelet analysis.

Rather than disintegrating the time series into smaller samples, as in the Fourier transform, the wavelet analysis produces scaled and shifted forms of a function by expanding the time series. An important virtue of the wavelet transform is the fact that it provides localised perspective of time series with endogenous variations of the wavelet lengths. Thus, in measuring movements at lower frequencies, the wavelet function expands whiles it shrinks when capturing movements at higher frequencies. Moreover, sudden or abrupt changes are inevitable in time series and wavelet is capable of adequately capturing such events by utilising short functions. Similarly, the wavelet approach is able to capture infrequent movements or movements that are persistent by utilising long functions

(Aguiar-Conraria et al., 2008). Crowley (2007) notes that the wavelet approach is capable of providing localisation in the components of a function as well as in time dimension, handle non-stationary data, provide decomposition of time series into various multiresolution constituents and examine fluctuations in macroeconomic series. The scales that are produced, following a decomposition, are necessarily a function of the number of observations (Crowley, 2007).

The fact that wavelet is capable of handling non-stationary time series data makes it all appropriate for this study. It would be counterproductive to test the stationarity properties of the data given that wavelet is capable of dealing with both stationary and non-stationary time series data. The current study relies on the works of Mensi et al. (2016) and Yang et al. (2018) who had used a wavelet-based quantile regression approach in other contexts. Wavelets of whatever form are defined as mother (ψ) wavelets and father (ϕ) wavelets and expressed as follows:

$\int \psi(t)dt = 0$ representing the mother wavelet, and
$\int \phi(t)dt = 1$ representing the father wavelet

That is, the father wavelets essentially integrate to 1 and they are designed to capture the trend of the series being decomposed. The father wavelets also capture the smooth part of the series or what is also regarded as the low-frequency component of the series under consideration. On the other hand, the mother wavelets integrate to zero; capture the high-frequency component of the series under consideration and represent aberrations from the trend.

Using wavelet transformation, the time series data denoted by $q(t)$ is decomposed as follows:

$$q(t) = \sum_k S_{J,k} \phi_{J,k}(t) + \sum_k c_{J,k} \psi_{J,k}(t) \sum_k c_{J-1,k} \psi_{J-1,k}(t) + \ldots$$
$$+ \sum_k c_{1,k} \psi_{1,k}(t) \tag{4.1}$$

with the wavelet functions defined by $\phi_{J,k}$ and $\psi_{J,k}$. Additionally, $S_{J,k}$ and $c_{J,k}$ up to $c_{1,k}$ are the wavelet transform's coefficients. Moreover, J implies the number of levels of the multiresolution, with k moving from 1 to the total coefficients at each of these levels. By way of representation, the wavelet transformation can be captured as:

$$S_{J,k} = \int \phi_{J,k}(t)q(t)dt \tag{4.2}$$

$$c_{j,k} = \int \psi_{j,k}(t)q(t)dt, \; with \; j \; moving \; from \; 1 \; to \; J \quad\quad (4.3)$$

so that J signifies greatest integer and 2^J takes a value below the total number of observations. Meanwhile, $S_{J,k}$ and $c_{J,k}$ up to $c_{1,k}$ respectively represent the coefficients of the trend and deviations from the trend. So, the original time series $q(t)$ can be approximated with the aid of the wavelet series as follows:

$$q(t)=S_{J,k}(t) + C_{J,k}(t) + C_{J-1,k}(t) + ...+ C_1(t) \quad\quad (4.4)$$

where $S_{J,k}(t)$ and $C_{J,k}(t)$ up to $C_1(t)$ respectively signify the trend and the detailed component of the signal that constitute aberrations from the trend. These detailed and trend components of the signal are defined respectively as

$$C_{J,k} = \sum_k c_{J,k}\psi_{J,k}(t), \; with \; j = 1 \; to \; J - 1 \; and \; S_{J,k} = \sum_k s_{J,k}\phi_{J,k}(t) \quad\quad (4.5)$$

The Discrete Wavelet Transform (DWT)

Aspects of the signal (the time series) representing the detailed components or high frequency, defined by $C_1(t)$ up to $C_J(t)$, are obtainable by deploying the wavelet filter's coefficients which scale the time series or initial signal in the form of $y = (y_{1,0}, ...,y_{1, L-1}, \; 0, ...,0)^T$. As $r_1 = (r_{1,0}, ...,r_{1, L-1}, \; 0, ...,0)^T$ captures the Daubechies wavelet filter coefficients (Daubechies, 1992), which are compactly supported for every unit scale that is zero-padded to **N** length such that for $l > L$, $r_{1,0} = 0$ subject to the following conditions:

$\sum_{l=0}^{L-1} r_{1,l} = 0$; $\sum_{l=0}^{L-1} r_{1,l}^2 = 1$ $\sum_{l=0}^{L-1} r_{1,l}h_{1,l+2n} = 0$ for all integers n which are not zero (Tiwari et al., 2013). Tiwari et al. (2013) reckoned that the rationale for the aforementioned condition is that a wavelet filter is supposed to have a unit energy; possess zero mean or its sum must be equal to 0; and must exhibit, to its own even shifts, orthogonality.

The expression $y_1 = (y_{1,0}, ...,y_{1, L-1}, \; 0, ...,0)^T$ can be denoted as scaling coefficients (zero-padded) with $y_{1,l} = (-1)^{l+1}r_{1,L-l-1}$. It is possible to also represent the time series as $m_0, ..., m_{N-1}$. The time series used in this study can be filtered by relying on r_j which produces the wavelets' coefficients for scales which have $N \geq L_j$ such that $L_j = (2^j - 1)(L - 1) + 1$. That is:

$$W_{j,t} = 2^{j/2} \hat{W}_{j,2^j(t+1)+1}, \quad \left[(L - 2)\left(1 - \frac{1}{2^j}\right) \right] \leq t \leq \left[\frac{N}{2^j} - 1 \right] \quad (4.6)$$

such that

$$\hat{W}_{j,t} = \frac{1}{2^{j/2}} \sum_{2^{j/2}}^{L_{j-1}} r_{j,l} M_{t-1}, \quad t = L_j - 1, \ldots \ldots N - 1$$

The coefficients of $\hat{W}_{j,t}$ related to variations on a scale with length $\pi_j = 2^{j-1}$ are obtained through the subsampling of each 2^jth of coefficients of $\hat{W}_{j,t}$.

The Maximal Overlap Discrete Wavelet Transform (MODWT)

The requirement that the sample size be divided by 2^j as well as the dynamic length requirement inherent in the DWT makes DWT rather limited and restrictive. As a result, this study employs the maximal overlap discrete wavelet transform (MODWT) as it is free from restrictions and limitations identified with DWT. Moreover, a significant downside of the DWT is that only sample sizes of multiples of two are compatible with the DWT. Such a limitation is non-existent with the MODWT as it can be utilised for any sample size. Additionally, it does not suffer phase-shifts that alter events' location in time (Mensi et al., 2016). Importantly, it does not change with respect to translations because the pattern of the coefficients of the wavelet transform does not vary following a signal shift. With the MODWT, the wavelets' coefficients captured by $\hat{W}_{j,t}$ as well as the coefficients of the scales defined by $\hat{V}_{j,t}$ where j varies from 1 to J are obtained as:

$$\hat{W}_{j,t} = \sum_{l=0}^{L-1} \hat{y}_l \, \hat{v}_{j-1,t \bmod N} \quad \text{and} \quad \hat{V}_{j,t} = \sum_{l=0}^{L-1} \hat{r} \hat{v}_{j-1, \, t-1 \bmod N} \quad (4.7)$$

The wavelet's filters are rescaled and scales ($\hat{y}_l$ and $\hat{r}_l$) as $\hat{y}_j = y_j/2^{j/2}$ and $\hat{r}_j = r_j/2^{j/2}$. Coefficients of the wavelets, which are not decimated, represent the dissimilarities between the data's generalised averages with the aid of a scale of $\pi_j = 2^{J-1}$.

The quantile regression

To ascertain the monetary policy effect on food inflation across different horizons and at various quantiles of the distribution of food prices in the selected economies, the quantile regression technique is applied to the decomposed series (from the wavelet). Relying on the works of Iddrisu & Alagidede (2020, 2021), the quantile regression approach is implemented as follows:

$$f_t = x'_t \beta + u_t \tag{4.8a}$$

$$E(f_t | x_t) = x'_t \beta \tag{4.8b}$$

$$Q_{f_t}(\pi | x_t) = x'_t \beta_\pi \tag{4.8c}$$

$$\beta_\pi = \beta + \varphi F^{-1}(\pi) \tag{4.8d}$$

where φ denotes a constant; the cumulative distribution function of $\{u_t\}$ is given by F; the quantiles of interest are defined by π; conditional quantile function of food inflation is denoted by $Q_{f_t}(\pi | x_t)$. With 149 observations for each country being studied, the specified quantiles are 25th, 50th and 75th. These splits allow sufficient observations at the specified quantiles for a meaningful inference. In the above equations, β_π signifies a vector of parameters to be computed at the specified quantiles. Error term is represented by u_t and the vector of the regressors is given by the x_t. In the main model, the impact of monetary policy on food prices is estimated for each country while controlling for real gross domestic product, exchange rate and the global food price inflation. For robustness purposes, another model is estimated where the main variables of interest (food inflation and monetary policy) are maintained but the control variables are varied. That is, real gross domestic product is dropped and, in its stead, real household consumption expenditure and real gross fixed capital formation are introduced.

To estimate the parameters in equation (4.8), a minimisation of the following loss function is performed:

$$\min_{\beta_\pi \in \Re^p} \sum_{t=1}^{T} \rho_\pi (f_t - x'_t \beta_\pi) \tag{4.9}$$

such that p = dimension (β_π). The loss function in equation (4.9) is simplified as:

$$\rho_\pi(u) = u(\pi - I(u < 0))$$

where I denotes an indicator function with a value of 1 when $u < 0$ or 0 if the reverse is the case.

With quantile regression, unlike mean-based techniques, the sum of the residuals' absolute values as well as the associated asymmetric penalties are minimised. As a result, the minimisation problem expressed in equation (4.9) can be captured as:

$$\min_{\beta_\pi \in \Re^p} \sum_{t=1}^{T} \pi|u_t| + \sum_{t=1}^{T} (1 - \pi)|u_t| \qquad (4.10)$$

where $\pi|u_t|$ captures the penalisation for $u_t \geq 0$, whereas $(1 - \theta)|u_t|$ penalises the case where $u_t < 0$.

Results

This section presents the empirical results. Given that the wavelet approach is much suited for time series data, the model is estimated for each country separately, rather than putting them together as a panel. The advantage is that it provides the complement of nuanced country-specific monetary policy-food inflation nexus. The presentation of the results in this section begins with the wavelet analysis. The time series data for each of the countries were decomposed into scales. The number of scales obtained, given the sample size of 149 observations, is four denoted by D1 to D4 (see Crowley, 2007 for detailed discussions on sample size and scales). The trend is then given by S4. In Table 4.1, the decompositions are defined in line with the work of Crowley (2007).

Table 4.1 Definition of scales

Scale (monthly)	Definition
D1	2 to 4 months
D2	4 to 8 months
D3	8 to 16 months
D4	16 to 32 months

At each of these scales and for each country, the monetary policy–food inflation relationship is estimated. The results are presented below under each country's heading.

Brazil

Results on Brazil are presented in Table 4.2. The results show that monetary policy effect on food prices in Brazil over the first- to the eighth-month horizon is statistically insignificant. From the eight-to-

Table 4.2 Results on Brazil

Scales	Variables	25th Quantile	50th Quantile	75th Quantile
D1	MPR	−0.154(0.170)	−0.192(0.165)	−0.090(0.145)
	RGDP	−0.00002**(9.47e-06)	−0.00002** (9.20e-06)	−0.000014* (8.03e-06)
	USD	−0.856(0.790)	−0.053(0.768)	−0.509(0.670)
	GFPI	−0.014(0.018)	−0.017(0.017)	−0.003(0.015)
	Constant	−0.135***(0.024)	0.0028(0.023)	0.158***(0.020)
	Pseudo R²	0.10	0.10	0.10
D2	MPR	−0.490(0.398)	−0.041(0.486)	−0.278(0.385)
	RGDP	−0.00005**(0.00002)	−0.00002(0.00002)	−0.00002(0.00002)
	USD	−0.887(1.004)	−1.196(1.226)	−2.004**(0.970)
	GFPI	0.0096(0.025)	−0.041(0.030)	−0.038(0.024)
	Constant	−0.415***(0.052)	0.011(0.063)	0.343***(0.050)
	Pseudo R²	0.10	0.10	0.10
D3	MPR	0.393*(0.216)	0.213(0.218)	0.425(0.266)
	RGDP	0.00002**(0.00001)	0.000018(0.000011)	0.000018(0.000014)
	USD	1.212(0.936)	−0.645(0.945)	−0.325(1.152)
	GFPI	−0.004(0.019)	−0.008(0.019)	0.030(0.023)
	Constant	−0.534***(0.072)	−0.081(0.073)	0.452***(0.089)
	Pseudo R²	0.04	0.02	0.05
D4	MPR	1.134***(0.139)	1.088***(0.137)	1.183***(0.210)
	RGDP	0.00003***(9.33e-06)	0.00003(9.20e-06)	0.000026* (0.000014)
	USD	4.273***(1.017)	5.014***(1.003)	4.215***(1.542)
	GFPI	0.103***(0.018)	0.109***(0.017)	0.092***(0.027)
	Constant	−0.771***(0.111)	−0.060(0.110)	0.682***(0.169)
	Pseudo R²	0.32	0.33	0.29
S4	MPR	0.578**(0.268)	0.977**(0.367)	−0.327(0.295)
	RGDP	0.00004***(6.36e-06)	0.00003*** (8.71e-06)	−2.73e-06(6.99e-06)
	USD	−4.358***(0.810)	−1.372(1.108)	2.953***(0.889)
	GFPI	−0.010(0.036)	−0.047(0.049)	0.050(0.039)
	Constant	−30.120***(7.332)	−27.121**(10.034)	9.459(8.054)
	Pseudo R²	0.35	0.11	0.10

Standard errors in parenthesis. *, **, and *** signify 10%, 5% and 1% significance level, respectively.

sixteen-month horizon (scale D3), however, monetary policy effect on food inflation becomes significant statistically but only at the 25th quantile of the distribution of food prices. Specifically, monetary policy tightening by a percentage point elicits 0.393% increase in food prices in Brazil at the 25th quantile. Over the sixteen-to-thirty-two-month horizon, monetary policy effect on food prices is positive and statistically significant at all the quantiles of food inflation. Specifically, a percentage monetary policy expansion leads to 1.134%, 1.088% and 1.183% decline in food prices at the 25th, 50th and 75th quantiles, respectively. Indeed, the trend (S4) also indicates that monetary policy effect on food prices is positive and statistically significant at all the quantiles.

The positive relationship between monetary policy and food inflation in Brazil is similar to the findings of Bhattacharya & Jain (2020) on the same country. Other studies that have found positive relationship between monetary policy and food inflation, but not necessarily in Brazil, include Iddrisu & Aagidede (2020, 2021) and Hammoudeh 2015. An explanation for the positive relationship between monetary policy and food inflation has been proffered in the literature. Bhattacharya & Jain (2020) argued that the cost of production of firms which produce non-food items sees an upturn when interest rates are increased (contraction in monetary policy). The cost of production of these firms increases because of their capital-intensive feature which makes them sensitive to interest rates. A rise in capital cost, relative to wages, incentivizes the deployment of more labour (seen to be cheaper) relative to capital. The switch to labour then puts upward pressure on wages. Meanwhile, firms that produce food items are known to be reliant on labour relative to capital. Upward wage pressures, precipitated by factor substitution in the non-food sector, increases the production cost of firms that produce food items, and the prices of food increase as a consequence.

This study argues that the positive relationship between monetary policy and food inflation may not always have to emanate from the non-food sector to the food sector as put forward by Bhattacharya & Jain (2020). The nature of modern agriculture, food production and the accompanying supply chain provide ample reason to expect the cost of production channel to be operative directly in the food sector but not necessarily emanate from the non-food sector. Farming in most emerging and advanced economies is now done on large commercial scale requiring substantial investments that include acquisition of heavy equipment. Such large-scale investments would naturally involve debt elements and so interest rate hikes naturally increase the production cost of these commercial farms and the effect trickles down to food prices eventually. Similarly, firms engaged in food processing also require substantial capital investments, making them sensitive to interest rates hikes. Given the fairly inelastic demand for food items, the incremental cost resulting from interest rate hikes is easily passed on to food prices. Moreover, and on the account of the same reasoning, food items from the food sector get to final consumers through the efforts of wholesalers and retailers who also invest heavily on transportation infrastructure, warehouses, packing and packaging equipment. These investments make the wholesalers and retailers sensitive to interest rates as well. Clearly, the transmission does not always have to emanate from the non-food sector to the food sector. The architecture of modern food production, the value chain and the supply dynamics provide a reasonable transmission channel. Indeed, the dominance of food in consumption baskets of most developing and emerging countries and the fairly inelastic demand for food items are probable reasons to expect a positive relationship between monetary policy and food prices. Unlike the non-food items that households can defer expenditure on, food represents an essential requirement of life. Large commercial farmers and firms will still borrow to invest in food processing and food production regardless of interest rate levels because such costs can easily be passed on to consumers in view of the demand inelasticity for food.

The fiscal dominance argument by Sargent & Wallace (1981) has also been mooted as a possible reason for the positive impact of monetary policy on food inflation (see Iddrisu & Alagidede, 2020).

The effect of real gross domestic product on food prices over the two-to-four-month horizon is negative and statistically significant across all the quantiles. In other words, declining real output levels in Brazil engender food prices increases over the two-to-four-month horizon. The direction of the results is not different over the four-to-eight-month horizon except that the effect of real gross domestic product is only statistically significant at the 25th quantile. Over the next two scales, however, the effect of real gross domestic product is positive but statistically significant only at the 25th quantile at scale D3 and at the 25th and 75th quantiles at scale D4. At scale D4 (sixteen-to-thirty-two-month horizon), the exchange rate effect on food prices is positive and statistically significant at all the quantiles. That is, a percentage depreciation of the Brazilian Real against the United States Dollar (increase in the exchange rate) elicits increases in food inflation by 4.273% at the 25th quantile, 5.014% at the median and 4.215% at the 75th quantile. In addition, the effect of global food prices on domestic food prices in Brazil at scale D4 is positive and statistically significant across all the quantiles. Specifically, when world food prices increase by 1%, domestic food prices in Brazil increase by 0.103% at the 25th quantile, 0.109% at the median and 0.092% at the 75th quantile. That is expected given the observed similar paths of the world food prices and domestic food prices in Brazil in chapter 3.

Chile

Over the two-to-four-month horizon (scale D1), monetary policy effect on food prices is positive but statistically significant only at the 25th quantile (see Table 4.3). A percentage restriction in monetary policy rate leads to an increase in food prices by 0.89% in Chile. At scale D2,

Table 4.3 Results on Chile

Scales	Variables	25th Quantile	50th Quantile	75th Quantile
D1	MPR	0.888*(0.524)	0.5791(0.4835)	0.4798(0.4376)
	RGDP	−9.12e-08(1.19e-07)	−2.31e-07**(1.10e-07)	−2.13e-07**(9.98e-08)
	USD	0.017**(0.0075)	0.0089(0.0069)	0.0123*(0.0063)
	GFPI	0.0671**(0.027)	0.0665***(0.0252)	0.092***(0.023)
	Constant	−0.192***(0.035)	0.002(0.033)	0.1878***(0.0296)
	Pseudo R^2	0.10	0.10	0.13
D2	MPR	0.4078(0.3829)	0.7812**(0.3661)	0.305(0.504)
	RGDP	−3.74e-07**(1.50e-07)	−2.68e-07*(1.43e-07)	−5.36e-07***(1.97e-07)
	USD	0.0316***(0.009)	0.0184**(0.0083)	0.0224*(0.0114)
	GFPI	0.0816**(0.033)	0.0503(0.0316)	0.1135**(0.0434)
	Constant	−0.4115***(0.0634)	−0.0553(0.0606)	0.394***(0.084)
	Pseudo R^2	0.114	0.10	0.10
D3	MPR	−0.3735(0.3908)	−0.5111(0.3599)	−0.2584(0.3151)
	RGDP	−7.03e-07***(2.07e-07)	−4.43e-07**(1.91e-07)	−3.30e-07**(1.67e-07)
	USD	0.0326**(0.0163)	0.0214(0.0150)	0.0255*(0.0132)
	GFPI	0.0528(0.0401)	0.0118(0.0369)	0.0327(0.0323)
	Constant	−0.6988***(0.1169)	0.0244(0.1076)	0.5976***(0.0942)
	Pseudo R^2	0.034	0.04	0.06
D4	MPR	1.8289***(0.2726)	1.5933***(0.2176)	1.4029***(0.2354)
	RGDP	7.23e-07***(2.25e-07)	5.63e-07***(1.80e-07)	6.47e-07***(1.94e-07)
	USD	−0.0360(0.0231)	−0.0645***(0.0184)	−0.0685***(0.0199)
	GFPI	−0.0484(0.0482)	−0.1059***(0.0384)	−0.0951**(0.0416)
	Constant	−0.8167***(0.1835)	0.0405(0.1466)	0.9102***(0.1585)
	Pseudo R^2	0.29	0.24	0.25
S4	MPR	1.0555***(0.3067)	2.2314***(0.1849)	2.4805***(0.2214)
	RGDP	1.40e-07(1.55e-07)	−5.99e-07***(9.37e-08)	−6.11e-07***(1.12e-07)
	USD	−0.0065(0.0081)	0.0192***(0.0049)	0.0335***(0.0059)
	GFPI	0.0570(0.0385)	0.0186(0.0232)	0.0455(0.0278)
	Constant	−1.2780(5.0888)	5.0189(3.0683)	−2.4293(3.6736)
	Pseudo R^2	0.26	0.40	0.50

Standard errors in parenthesis. *, **, and *** signify 10%, 5% and 1% significance level, respectively.

monetary policy effect on food prices is positive but significant statistically at the median. That is, food prices increase by 0.78% at the
median following a percentage increase in the monetary policy rate in
Chile. At scale D3, monetary policy effect on food prices is not statistically significant. At scale D4, monetary policy effect on food prices
is positive and statistically significant at all the quantiles of food inflation. Specifically, food prices increase by 1.83%, 1.59% and 1.4% at
the 25th, 50th and 75th quantiles respectively following a percentage
restriction in monetary policy. Essentially, the destabilization in food
prices in Chile, following monetary policy restriction is greater over
the longer horizons. Indeed, the trend (S4) in the monetary policy
effect on food prices gives credence to this assertion.

The effect of real gross domestic product on food prices at scale D1,
although very marginal, is negative and statistically significant across
all the quantiles. The exchange rate effect on food prices at the same
scale (D1) is positive and statistically significant at the 25th and the
75th quantiles. Specifically, a percentage appreciation of the Chilean
Peso against the United States Dollar (decline in exchange rate) leads
to decrease in food prices by 0.017% and 0.012% at the 25th and the
75th quantiles, respectively. Unlike Brazil where the pass through of
global food prices to domestic prices is statistically significant only
over a long horizon (D4), changes in global food prices exert statistically significant effect on domestic prices in Chile over the short-term
horizon of two-to-four months (scale D1). A percentage increase in
global food prices elicits a 0.067%, 0.067% and 0.092% increase in
domestic food prices in Chile at the 25th, 50th and 75th quantiles,
respectively. At scale D2, the effect of real gross domestic product on
food prices is negative and statistically significant across all the
quantiles. The effect of exchange rate on food prices at scale D2 is also
positive and statistically significant at all the quantiles. Food prices
drop by 0.032%, 0.018% and 0.022% at the 25th, 50th and 75th
quantiles following a percentage appreciation of the Peso against the
Dollar. The effect of global food prices is positive but statistically
significant at the 25th and 75th quantiles. Domestic food prices fall by
0.082% and 0.114% at the 25th and 75th quantiles respectively following a percentage decline in the world food prices. At scale D3, the
output effect on food prices is negative and statistically significant
at all the quantiles. Similarly, the effect of exchange rate is also positive
and statistically significant at the 25th and 75th quantiles. A percentage depreciation of the Peso sees an increase in domestic food
prices in Chile by 0.033% and 0.026% at the 25th and 75th quantiles,
respectively.

Colombia

For Colombia, we find that monetary policy effect on food prices is mixed (see Table 4.4). Over the short horizon (scale D1 or two-to-four-month horizon), monetary policy impact on food prices is negative but statistically significant only at the 75th quantile. Specifically, a monetary policy tightening by 1% elicits 0.701% decline in food prices in Colombia over the short horizon. From scales D2 to D4, however, monetary policy effect on food prices is positive and statistically significant. At scale D2, monetary policy effect on food prices is positive but significant statistically only at the 25th quantile. That is, food prices increase by 2.4341% at the 25th quantile following a percentage restriction in monetary policy. At scale D3, monetary policy effect on

Table 4.4 Results on Colombia

Scales	Variables	25th Quantile	50th Quantile	75th Quantile
D1	MPR	−0.4757(0.4189)	−0.2725(0.2511)	−0.7009**(0.3209)
	RGDP	−1.06e-07***(2.34e-08)	−9.43e-08***(1.40e-08)	−1.00e-07***(1.79e-08)
	USD	−0.0209*(0.0120)	−0.0086(0.0072)	−0.0101(0.0092)
	GFPI	0.0094(0.0340)	0.0054(0.0204)	−0.0178(0.0261)
	Constant	−0.1973***(0.0465)	0.0233(0.0278)	0.1894***(0.0356)
	Pseudo R^2	0.11	0.10	0.12
D2	MPR	2.4341***(0.7049)	1.2372(0.9698)	0.2341(1.0050)
	RGDP	−3.51e-08(2.75e-08)	−4.39e-08(3.79e-08)	−6.83e-08(3.93e-08)
	USD	−0.0059(0.0101)	0.0083(0.0139)	−0.0078(0.0144)
	GFPI	−0.0723**(0.0277)	−0.0355(0.0381)	−0.0583(0.0395)
	Constant	−0.5042***(0.0570)	−0.0076(0.0785)	0.3707***(0.0813)
	Pseudo R^2	0.12	0.10	0.10
D3	MPR	1.6554***(0.5692)	1.3448***(0.3484)	1.8955***(0.6725)
	RGDP	−2.13e-08(3.29e-08)	−5.26e-08**(2.01e-08)	−3.47e-08(3.88e-08)
	USD	0.0124(0.0124)	0.0124(0.0076)	0.0037(0.0146)
	GFPI	−0.0408(0.0287)	−0.0400**(0.0176)	−0.0544(0.0339)
	Constant	−0.5360***(0.1092)	−0.0806(0.0668)	0.5121***(0.1290)
	Pseudo R^2	0.17	0.21	0.19
D4	MPR	2.5531***(0.1988)	2.3520***(0.2929)	2.5181***(0.3759)
	RGDP	−4.01e-08**(1.91e-08)	−1.94e-08(2.81e-08)	2.87e-09(3.61e-08)
	USD	0.0037(0.0154)	0.0176(0.0228)	−0.0292(0.0292)
	GFPI	−0.0450**(0.0174)	−0.0215(0.0256)	−0.0524(0.0328)
	Constant	−0.7951(0.0943)	−0.1976(0.1390)	0.8764***(0.1784)
	Pseudo R^2	0.31	0.25	0.28
S4	MPR	1.8508***(0.1182)	1.8683***(0.2034)	1.788***(0.2100)
	RGDP	−9.25e-09(1.23e-08)	3.74e-08*(2.11e-08)	1.20e-07***(2.18e-08)
	USD	−0.0201***(0.0061)	−0.0019(0.0105)	0.0081(0.0108)
	GFPI	−0.0415**(0.0176)	−0.0391(0.0302)	−0.0064(0.0312)
	Constant	−4.2217**(1.9863)	−11.0310***(3.4182)	−21.2976***(3.5291)
	Pseudo R^2	0.50	0.49	0.53

Standard errors in parenthesis. *, **, and *** signify 10%, 5% and 1% significance level, respectively.

food prices is positive and statistically significant across all the quantiles. Specifically, food prices increase by 1.655%, 1.345% and 1.896% at the 25th, 50th and 75th quantiles respectively following a percentage increase in the monetary policy rate. Similarly, the effect of monetary policy at scale D4 on food prices is positive and statistically significant across all the quantiles. An increase in monetary policy rate by 1% engenders increase in food prices by 2.55%, 2.35% and 2.52% at the 25th, 50th and 75th quantiles, respectively. The findings on monetary policy show that the stabilisation in food prices following monetary policy tightening in Colombia is possible only over a short horizon. Over a longer horizon, monetary policy tightening is rather destabilising. Indeed, the long-term trend indicates that monetary policy effect on food prices is positive across all the quantiles.

At scales D1, D3 and D4, the effect of real gross domestic product on food prices in Colombia is negative but statistically significant across all the quantiles at D1, at the median at D3 and the 25th quantile at D4. For the exchange rate effect on food prices, it is negative but significant statistically only at the 25th quantile at scale D1. That is, a percentage appreciation of the Colombian Peso against the United States Dollar at scale D1 elicits an increase of 0.021% in food prices at the 25th quantile. On the effect of global food prices on domestic food prices in Colombia, it is found that the effect is negative at scales D2, D3 and D4. At scale D2, the negative effect of global food prices is statistically significant only at the 25th quantile. Thus, a percentage rise in global food prices sees a 0.072% decline in domestic food prices at the 25th quantile in Colombia. At scale D3, the effect of global food prices on domestic food prices is significant only at the median. Domestic food prices reduce by 0.04% at the median following a percentage increase in global food prices. At scale D4, global food prices exert a statistically significant impact on domestic prices in Colombia only at the 25th quantile. At that quantile, domestic food prices decline by 0.045% following a percent increase in global food prices.

Ghana

Monetary policy effect on food prices in Ghana is found to be positive and statistically significant only at the 75th quantile at scale D3 (see Table 4.5). Food prices increase by 0.7599% at the 75th quantile of scale D3 following a percentage tightening in monetary policy. At scale D4, monetary policy effect on food prices is positive and statistically significant across all the quantiles. Specifically, food prices increase by

Table 4.5 Results on Ghana

Scales	Variables	25th Quantile	50th Quantile	75th Quantile
D1	MPR	−0.0253(0.2745)	−0.0584(0.1430)	−0.2711(0.1776)
	RGDP	−7.73e-11(7.51e-11)	−5.65e-11(3.92e-11)	−8.29e-11*(4.86e-11)
	USD	0.3744(1.7394)	0.0159(0.9065)	1.1043(1.1253)
	GFPI	0.0396(0.0468)	0.0158(0.0244)	0.1086***(0.0303)
	Constant	−0.1938(0.0628)	−0.0092(0.0327)	0.2300***(0.0406)
	Pseudo R^2	0.05	0.06	0.09
D2	MPR	0.1075(0.3002)	0.1258(0.2279)	0.2635(0.2688)
	RGDP	3.09e-11(8.59e-11)	−2.08e-11(6.52e-11)	3.23e-11(7.69e-11)
	USD	−1.6036(2.0035)	−0.3912(1.5212)	−2.0507(1.7939)
	GFPI	−0.0334(0.0311)	−0.0313(0.0236)	−0.0620**(0.0279)
	Constant	−0.3040***(0.0678)	−0.0090(0.0515)	0.3013***(0.0607)
	Pseudo R^2	0.04	0.04	0.06
D3	MPR	0.5424(0.3553)	0.3720(0.2256)	0.7599***(0.2813)
	RGDP	1.03e-11(9.86e-11)	−6.65e-11(6.26e-11)	−1.21e-10(7.81e-11)
	USD	−2.4657(2.2155)	−0.0081(1.4068)	0.8741(1.7546)
	GFPI	0.0207(0.0280)	0.0453**(0.0178)	0.0295(0.0222)
	Constant	−0.5670***(0.1131)	0.0513(0.0718)	0.5381***(0.0896)
	Pseudo R^2	0.12	0.13	0.15
D4	MPR	0.8307***(0.2102)	0.9645***(0.0988)	0.7325***(0.1531)
	RGDP	2.23e-10***(5.87e-11)	2.00e-10***(2.76e-11)	1.68e-10***(4.28e-11)
	USD	−6.0934***(1.3314)	−5.9915***(0.6255)	−5.4684***(0.9697)
	GFPI	−0.0331***(0.0116)	−0.0411***(0.0054)	−0.03937***(0.0084)
	Constant	−0.2885***(0.1020)	0.0484(0.0479)	0.3832***(0.0743)
	Pseudo R^2	0.36	0.45	0.45
S4	MPR	1.0526***(0.0850)	1.0234***(0.2071)	1.1734***(0.1981)
	RGDP	−7.93e-11(1.81e-11)	−1.02e-10**(4.41e-11)	−1.47e-10***(4.21e-11)
	USD	−3.2216***(0.5267)	−2.2931*(1.2833)	−1.5196(1.2274)
	GFPI	−0.0683***(0.0131)	−0.0683**(0.0319)	−0.0317(0.0305)
	Constant	4.4371**(1.9902)	6.7060(4.8495)	9.4211**(4.6381)
	Pseudo R^2	0.37	0.30	0.45

Standard errors in parenthesis. *, **, and *** signify 10%, 5% and 1% significance level, respectively.

0.831%, 0.965% and 0.733% at the 25th, 50th and 75th quantiles respectively following a percentage restriction in monetary policy. The positive effect of monetary on food inflation in Ghana is similar to the findings by Iddrisu & Alagidede (2021).

The results show that the effect of global food prices on domestic food prices in Ghana is mixed. The effect is positive at scales D1 and D3, but negative at scales D2 and D4. At scale D1, the effect is significant only at the 75th quantile. Food prices in Ghana decline by 0.11% at the 75th quantile at scale D1 following a percentage decrease in global food prices. At scale D2, food prices in Ghana decline by 0.062% at the 75th quantile following a percentage increase in the world food prices. At scale D3, global food prices exert a statistically significant positive impact on food prices only at the median. Food prices in Ghana decline by 0.045% following a percentage fall in the global food prices. At scale D4, food prices in Ghana increase by 0.033%, 0.041% and 0.039% at the 25th, 50th and the 75th quantiles respectively following a percentage decline in the world food prices.

Hungary

In Hungary, the results show that the effect of monetary policy on food inflation is positive and statistically significant at all the quantiles over the longer horizons or D3 and D4 scales (see Table 4.6). At scale D3, it is found that a percentage tightening of monetary policy elicits increases in food inflation by 1.294%, 2.883% and 2.201% at the 25th, 50th and 75th quantiles, respectively. The destabilization is even greater over the longer horizons (scale D4) as a percentage tightening of monetary policy leads to food inflation increases of 2.086%, 3.007% and 3.408% at the 25th, 50th and 75th quantiles, respectively. The long-term trend (S4) also shows a positive relationship between monetary policy and food prices.

The real gross domestic product exerts a positive effect on food prices in Hungary at all the scales, although the effect is marginal across the quantiles. It is also found that the global food prices impact domestic food prices positively in Hungary at all the scales. At scale D1, the positive effect is significant only at the median. That is, domestic food prices in Hungary decline by 0.051% at the median following a percentage decline in the global food prices. At scale D2, the positive effect of the global food prices is significant at the 25th and 50th quantiles. At the 25th quantile, domestic food prices increase by 0.096% following a percentage increase in global food prices. However, domestic food prices drop by 0.055% at the median following a percentage decline in global food prices. At scales D3 and D4, global food prices exert statistically significant positive effect on domestic food prices across all the quantiles. At scale D3, domestic food prices increase by 0.125%, 0.115% and 0.142% at the 25th, 50th and 75th quantiles respectively following a percentage increase in the global food prices. For scale D4, domestic food prices drop by 0.153%, 0.165% and 0.148% at the 25th, 50th and 75th quantiles respectively following a percentage fall in global food prices.

Indonesia

Monetary policy effect on food inflation in Indonesia is found to be mixed (see Table 4.7). At scale D2, the monetary policy effect is

Table 4.6 Results on Hungary

Scales	Variables	25th Quantile	50th Quantile	75th Quantile
D1	MPR	0.3409(0.3560)	0.1762(0.2926)	0.1367(0.3383)
	RGDP	2.29e-06(1.78e-06)	2.76e-06*(1.46e-06)	1.86e-06(1.69e-06)
	USD	−0.0158(0.0152)	−0.0258**(0.0125)	−0.0119(0.0144)
	GFPI	0.0405(0.0305)	0.0514**(0.0251)	0.0314(0.0290)
	Constant	−0.2328***(0.0415)	0.0187(0.0341)	0.2071***(0.0394)
	Pseudo R^2	0.03	0.05	0.03
D2	MPR	−0.1524(0.3883)	−0.2214(0.3466)	0.4894(0.3823)
	RGDP	6.95e-07(1.87e-06)	8.69e-08(1.67e-06)	3.38e-06*(1.84e-06)
	USD	−0.0201(0.0194)	−0.0274(0.0173)	−0.0476**(0.0191)
	GFPI	0.0957***(0.0348)	0.0551*(0.0310)	0.0443(0.0342)
	Constant	−0.3618***(0.0689)	0.0105(0.0615)	0.3682***(0.0678)
	Pseudo R^2	0.09	0.06	0.07
D3	MPR	1.2942**(0.6102)	2.8826***(0.4976)	2.2005***(0.5809)
	RGDP	5.23e-06***(1.87e-06)	0.000011***(1.52e-06)	7.53e-06***(1.78e-06)
	USD	−0.0030(0.0181)	−0.0162(0.0147)	−0.0076(0.0172)
	GFPI	0.1251***(0.0301)	0.1154***(0.0246)	0.1418***(0.0287)
	Constant	−0.5462***(0.0994)	−0.0240(0.0810)	0.5106***v(0.0946)
	Pseudo R^2	0.18	0.18	0.21
D4	MPR	2.0859***(0.3919)	3.0070***(0.4758)	3.4083***(0.3883)
	RGDP	8.37e-06***(1.67e-06)	0.000011***(2.03e-06)	0.000012***(1.66e-06)
	USD	0.0255(0.0222)	0.0386(0.0270)	0.0233(0.0220)
	GFPI	0.1525***(0.0256)	0.1652***(0.0311)	0.1481***(0.0254)
	Constant	−0.9305***(0.1284)	−0.0012(0.1559)	0.9891***(0.1273)
	Pseudo R^2	0.22	0.23	0.32
S4	MPR	1.2635***(0.1514)	1.8402***(0.2518)	2.2030***(0.1198)
	RGDP	5.28e-06***(6.28e-07)	4.34e-06***(1.04e-06)	5.49e-06***(4.97e-07)
	USD	−0.0144(0.0149)	0.0281(0.0248)	0.0203*(0.0118)
	GFPI	0.1601***(0.0177)	0.1532***(0.0294)	0.1024***(0.0140)
	Constant	−38.527***(4.909)	−42.302***(8.1616)	−49.567***(3.8835)
	Pseudo R^2	0.63	0.67	0.75

Standard errors in parenthesis. *, **, and *** signify 10%, 5% and 1% significance level, respectively.

positive but statistically significant only at the 25th and 50th quantiles. Specifically, food inflation increases by 2.56% and 2.77% at the 25th and 50th quantiles respectively following a percentage restriction in monetary policy. At scale D3, monetary policy tightening exerts negative effect on food prices but is only statistically significant at the 50th and 75th quantiles. At the 50th quantile, a percentage monetary policy tightening reduces food inflation by 0.68%. At the 75th quantile, food inflation drops by 0.86% following a percentage monetary policy restriction. At scale D4, monetary policy tightening exerts positive effect on food inflation at the 25th and 50th quantiles. Food prices increase by 0.173% and 0.172% at the 25th and 50th quantiles respectively following a percentage restriction in monetary policy.

Table 4.7 Results on Indonesia

Scales	Variables	25th Quantile	50th Quantile	75th Quantile
D1	MPR	0.8361(1.0622)	0.3066(1.2744)	1.5903(1.2080)
	RGDP	2.61e-10(6.72e-09)	−3.83e-09(8.06e-09)	4.69e-09(7.64e-09)
	USD	−0.0066(0.0060)	−0.0039(0.0072)	−0.0095(0.0068)
	GFPI	−0.0241(0.0422)	−0.0251(0.0507)	−0.0400(0.0480)
	Constant	−0.4121***(0.0571)	0.0186(0.0685)	0.3780***(0.0649)
	Pseudo R^2	0.03	0.05	0.06
D2	MPR	2.5555*(1.3226)	2.7665*(1.4215)	1.7890(1.2677)
	RGDP	1.50e-08*(8.99e-09)	1.65e-08*(9.67e-09)	9.05e-09(8.62e-09)
	USD	0.0304***(0.0106)	0.0250**(0.0114)	0.0194*(0.0101)
	GFPI	−0.0447(0.0500)	−0.0431(0.05373)	−0.0698(0.0479)
	Constant	−0.5488***(0.1086)	−0.0671(0.1167)	0.7002***(0.1041)
	Pseudo R^2	0.06	0.08	0.05
D3	MPR	−0.3241(0.2169)	−0.6766***(0.2410)	−0.8552***(0.2158)
	RGDP	−1.40e-09(1.67e-09)	−4.26e-09**(1.85e-09)	−4.96e-09***(1.66e-09)
	USD	0.0179***(0.0035)	0.0158***(0.0039)	0.0128***(0.0035)
	GFPI	−0.0421***(0.0103)	−0.0490***(0.0114)	−0.0553***(0.0102)
	Constant	−0.2553***(0.0386)	0.0215(0.0428)	0.2720***(0.0384)
	Pseudo R^2	0.14	0.14	0.16
D4	MPR	0.1726**(0.0681)	0.1724**(0.0821)	0.0479(0.0547)
	RGDP	1.70e-09***(6.11e-10)	1.77e-09**(7.37e-10)	1.07e-09**(4.91e-10)
	USD	0.0086***(0.0015)	0.0070***(0.0018)	0.0087***(0.0012)
	GFPI	−0.0002(0.0034)	0.0088**(0.0041)	0.0078***(0.0028)
	Constant	−0.2002***(0.0252)	0.0044(0.0304)	0.1720***(0.0202)
	Pseudo R^2	0.28	0.24	0.29
S4	MPR	0.1089***(0.0226)	0.1012***(0.0254)	0.1239***(0.0120)
	RGDP	1.30e-10(1.31e-10)	−2.01e-11(1.48e-10)	1.41e-10*(6.97e-11)
	USD	0.0033***(0.0010)	0.0031***(0.0011)	0.0053***(0.0005)
	GFPI	0.0031(0.0020)	0.0071***(0.0023)	0.0088***(0.0011)
	Constant	−0.7412*(0.4416)	−0.2469(0.4962)	−0.7535***(0.2344)
	Pseudo R^2	0.39	0.39	0.49

Standard errors in parenthesis. *, **, and *** signify 10%, 5% and 1% significance level, respectively.

The real gross domestic product exerts positive effect on food prices in Indonesia at the 25th and 50th quantiles at scale D2. The exchange rate also exerts positive effect on food prices at scale D2. A percentage depreciation in the Indonesian Rupiah against the United States Dollar (increase in the exchange rate) leads to food price increases of 0.03%, 0.025% and 0.019% at the 25th, 50th and 75th quantiles, respectively. Similarly at scale D3, the exchange rate impacts food prices positively in Indonesia across all the quantiles. A percentage appreciation of the Rupiah against the Dollar reduces food prices by 0.018%, 0.016% and 0.013% at the 25th, 50th and 75th quantiles, respectively. Meanwhile, the global food prices exert negative effect on domestic food prices in Indonesia across all the quantiles at scale D3. Domestic food prices fall by 0.042%, 0.049% and 0.055% at the 25th, 50th and 75th quantiles respectively following a percentage surge in global food prices. At scale D4, real gross domestic product impacts food prices positively across all quantiles. The exchange rate of the Rupiah to the Dollar also exerts positive effect on food prices across all the quantiles. Food prices drop by 0.009%, 0.007% and 0.009% at the 25th, 50th and 75th quantiles respectively following an appreciation of the Rupiah against the Dollar. Moreover, global food prices impact domestic prices positively at the median and 75th quantile. A percentage surge in the global food prices sees domestic food prices increasing by 0.0088% and 0.0078% at the median and 75th quantile.

Mexico

The results on Mexico show that monetary policy exerts positive impact on food inflation over the long horizon (D4). At that scale, monetary policy effect is positive and statistically significant across all the quantiles. A percentage restriction in monetary policy increases food inflation by 0.309% at the 25th quantile, 0.254% at the median and 0.228% at the 75th quantile (see Table 4.8). The long-term trend (S4) also indicates that the monetary policy exerts positive and significant effect on food prices across all the quantiles. The positive effect is similar to the findings of Bhattacharya & Jain (2020) on Mexico.

Real gross domestic product impacts food prices negatively at scales D1 and D2 but only significantly so at the 75th quantile at both scales. At scale D4, real gross domestic product impacts food inflation negatively at both the median and the 75th quantile. Global food prices impact domestic food prices in Mexico negatively but the effect is statistically significant at the 25th quantile and the median at scale D2. That is, a percentage increase in global food prices sees domestic food prices reduce by 0.043% and 0.070% at the 25th and 50th quantiles, respectively. The exchange rate of the Mexican Peso to the United States Dollar impacts food prices positively but only at the 25th quantile at scale D2. A percentage depreciation of the Mexican Peso leads 0.24% increase in food prices in Mexico.

Russia

Turning to Russia (Table 4.9), it is found that monetary policy effect on food inflation is positive and significant at various quantiles at all

Table 4.8 Results on Mexico

Scales	Variables	25th Quantile	50th Quantile	75th Quantile
D1	MPR	0.1861(1.1611)	0.9047(0.9404)	1.5324(1.0729)
	RGDP	−6.03e-06(4.73e-06)	−3.16e-06(3.83e-06)	−8.00e-06*(4.37e-06)
	USD	0.1329(0.4382)	−0.0204(0.3549)	0.4073(0.4049)
	GFPI	−0.0341(0.0453)	−0.0248(0.0367)	−0.0333(0.0419)
	Constant	−0.3222***(0.0615)	−0.0185(0.0498)	0.2635***(0.0569)
	Pseudo R^2	0.03	0.04	0.06
D2	MPR	−0.4461(0.8408)	−0.5960(0.8468)	−0.9862(0.7929)
	RGDP	2.37e-07(2.73e-06)	−1.39e-06(2.75e-06)	−4.28e-06*(2.57e-06)
	USD	−0.0151(0.2565)	0.0528(0.2584)	0.2245(0.2419)
	GFPI	−0.0433*(0.0257)	−0.0704***(0.0259)	−0.0358(0.0243)
	Constant	−0.3129***(0.0555)	−0.0528(0.0559)	0.3579***(0.0523)
	Pseudo R^2	0.04	0.03	0.06
D3	MPR	−0.3594(0.3205)	0.0651(0.2793)	−0.1016(0.3574)
	RGDP	−4.99e-07(1.43e-06)	3.49e-07(1.24e-06)	−6.09e-07(1.59e-06)
	USD	0.2384*(0.1409)	0.0531(0.1227)	0.2130(0.1571)
	GFPI	0.0036(0.0127)	−0.0082(0.0111)	−0.0085(0.0142)
	Constant	−0.2770***(0.0521)	−0.0241(0.0454)	0.3028***(0.0581)
	Pseudo R^2	0.06	0.03	0.03
D4	MPR	0.3094***(0.1045)	0.2536***(0.0748)	0.2275***(0.0697)
	RGDP	−5.94e-07(6.80e-07)	−8.31e-07*(4.86e-07)	−9.31e-07**(4.54e-07)
	USD	0.0170(0.0838)	0.0161(0.0600)	−0.0323(0.0559)
	GFPI	−0.0034(0.0048)	0.0006(0.0034)	−0.0011(0.0032)
	Constant	−0.1348***(0.0276)	0.0136(0.0198)	0.1264***(0.0184)
	Pseudo R^2	0.05	0.13	0.14
S4	MPR	0.0290*(0.0149)	0.0770***(0.0128)	0.1019***(0.0097)
	RGDP	2.98e-07*(1.61e-07)	2.96e-07**(1.39e-07)	1.64e-07(1.05e-07)
	USD	−0.0230(0.0170)	−0.0261*(0.0146)	−0.0136(0.0111)
	GFPI	0.0034*(0.0020)	−0.0014(0.0017)	−0.0042***(0.0013)
	Constant	−0.5540(0.4252)	−0.6265*(0.3662)	−0.3525(0.2778)
	Pseudo R^2	0.08	0.20	0.29

Standard errors in parenthesis. *, **, and *** signify 10%, 5% and 1% significance level, respectively.

the scales (D1 to D4). At scale D1, monetary policy effect on food prices is positive but statistically significant only at the median. Specifically, food prices surge by 0.201% at the median following a percentage monetary policy restriction. At scale D2, monetary policy

Table 4.9 Results on Russia

Scales	Variables	25th Quantile	50th Quantile	75th Quantile
D1	MPR	0.0273(0.1358)	0.2012**(0.0908)	0.0477(0.1543)
	RGDP	−2.20e−06***(7.81e-07)	−2.44e−06***(5.23e-07)	−2.11e-06**(8.88e-07)
	USD	−0.0601(0.0654)	0.0062(0.0437)	−0.0307(0.0743)
	GFPI	−0.0200(0.0284)	−0.0184(0.0190)	−0.0121(0.0322)
	Constant	−0.2072***(0.0389)	−0.0069(0.0260)	0.1661***(0.0442)
	Pseudo R^2	0.15	0.14	0.14
D2	MPR	0.1906(0.2092)	0.1760(0.1846)	0.5363**(0.2079)
	RGDP	−3.42e−06***(9.64e-07)	−4.36e−06***(8.50e-07)	−3.76e−06***(9.57e-07)
	USD	0.0053(0.0611)	0.1119**(0.0539)	0.0598(0.0607)
	GFPI	0.0293(0.0358)	−0.0099(0.0315)	−0.0288(0.0355)
	Constant	−0.4397***(0.0774)	0.0173(0.0683)	0.4586***(0.0769)
	Pseudo R^2	0.15	0.13	0.17
D3	MPR	0.5780(0.3764)	0.4207*(0.2338)	0.5144*(0.2986)
	RGDP	−2.18e-06(1.59e-06)	−2.56e-06**(9.89e-07)	−2.64e-06**(1.26e-06)
	USD	0.0343(0.1139)	0.0073(0.0707)	0.0672(0.0903)
	GFPI	0.1102***(0.0345)	0.1278***(0.0214)	0.1359***(0.0274)
	Constant	−0.5458***(0.1444)	0.0844(0.0897)	0.6770***(0.1146)
	Pseudo R^2	0.23	0.27	0.30
D4	MPR	2.2848***(0.3689)	2.0463***(0.3227)	2.4103***(0.3000)
	RGDP	−1.74e-07(1.61e-06)	1.49e-06(1.41e-06)	2.07e-06(1.31e-06)
	USD	−0.2142(0.1570)	−0.0389(0.1373)	−0.1493(0.1277)
	GFPI	0.0810*(0.0422)	0.1210***(0.0369)	0.1483***(0.0343)
	Constant	−1.9531***(0.2866)	0.1101(0.2507)	1.545**(0.2331)
	Pseudo R^2	0.25	0.31	0.35
S4	MPR	4.6777***(0.2868)	3.962***(0.2722)	3.3834***(0.2686)
	RGDP	6.86e-06***(7.12e-07)	6.59e-06***(6.75e-07)	4.98e-06***(6.66e-07)
	USD	−0.3770***(0.0369)	−0.3805***(0.0350)	−0.2752***(0.0346)
	GFPI	−0.0131(0.0302)	0.0072(0.0287)	0.0922***(0.0283)
	Constant	−111.47***(10.226)	−99.03***(9.7029)	−74.866***(9.5750)
	Pseudo R^2	0.41	0.49	0.60

Standard errors in parenthesis. *, **, and *** signify 10%, 5% and 1% significance level, respectively.

impact on food inflation is positive but statistically significant only at the 75th quantile where food prices increase by 0.536% following a percentage increase in monetary policy rate. At scale D3, the positive monetary policy effect on food prices is statistically significant at the median and the 75th quantile. Food prices rise by 0.421% and 0.514% at the median and the 75th quantile respectively following a percentage monetary policy restriction. At scale D4 (longer horizon), the positive monetary policy effect on food prices magnifies and is statistically significant across all the quantiles. Food prices increase by 2.285%, 2.046% and 2.410% at the 25th, 50th and the 75th quantiles respectively following a percentage contraction in monetary policy.

The effect of real gross domestic product on food prices is negative and statistically significant at scales D1 to D3. At scale D2, the exchange rate of the Russian Ruble against the United States Dollar has a positive effect on food prices but statistically significant only at the median. An appreciation of the Ruble by a percentage point reduces food prices by 0.112% at the median. Global food prices exert positive impact on domestic food prices in Russia at scales D3 and D4. At scale D3, the effect of global food prices on the domestic food prices is statistically significant at all the quantiles. When global food prices increase by 1% at scale D3, domestic food prices increase by 0.1102%, 0.1128% and 0.1359% at the 25th, 50th and 75th quantiles, respectively. Similarly, at scale D4, a percentage increase in global food prices increases domestic food prices by 0.081%, 0.121% and 0.148% at the 25th, 50th and 75th quantiles, respectively.

South Africa

For South Africa, the results show that monetary policy effect on food inflation is positive and statistically significant at scale D2 and specifically at the median. At scale D2, a percentage monetary policy restriction elicits a 0.724% increase in food prices at the median in South Africa (see Table 4.10). At scale D4, monetary policy exerts positive impact on food prices across all the quantiles. A contraction in monetary policy at scale D4 sees an increase in food prices by 0.087%, 0.163% and 0.178% at the 25th, 50th and 75th quantiles, respectively. The long-term trend (S4) also shows that monetary policy exerts positive impact on food prices in South Africa. The findings of positive monetary policy effect on food inflation in South Africa is akin to the findings by Iddrisu & Alagidede (2020) on the same country.

At scales D3 and D4, the effect of real gross domestic product on food inflation is negative and significant statistically across all quantiles. The exchange rate of the South African Rand to the United States Dollar exerts a positive effect on food prices in South Africa at scale D3. At that scale, a percentage depreciation of the Rand against the Dollar sees an increase in food prices in South Africa by 0.557%, 0.416% and 0.397% at the 25th, 50th and 75th quantiles, respectively. Meanwhile, the effect of the global food prices on the domestic food prices in South Africa at that scale (D3) is also positive but significant statistically only at the median where domestic food prices drop by 0.014% following a percentage decline in the world food prices. At scale D4, a percentage depreciation of the Rand elicits increases of 0.302%, 0.299% and 0.321% at the 25th,

Table 4.10 Results on South Africa

Scales	Variables	25th Quantile	50th Quantile	75th Quantile
D1	MPR	−0.3077(0.4878)	−0.1787(0.3580)	−0.0219(0.4821)
	RGDP	1.04e-12(3.69e-12)	−7.10e-15(2.71e-12)	−2.36e-13(3.65e-12)
	USD	−0.2274(0.3497)	−0.2413(0.2566)	−0.0988(0.3456)
	GFPI	−0.0067(0.0366)	−0.0104(0.0269)	0.0007(0.0362)
	Constant	−0.2263***(0.0496)	−0.0060(0.0364)	0.2113***(0.0490)
	Pseudo R^2	0.02	0.03	0.015
D2	MPR	0.4891(0.3863)	0.7242**(0.2998)	0.2675(0.3624)
	RGDP	−3.24e-13(1.68e-12)	2.52e-13(1.30e-12)	−3.89e-13(1.58e-12)
	USD	−0.0669(0.1449)	−0.0290(0.1124)	−0.0602(0.1359)
	GFPI	0.0051(0.0138)	−0.0030(0.0107)	0.0024(0.0130)
	Constant	−0.1733***(0.0295)	−0.0297(0.0229)	0.1641***(0.0276)
	Pseudo R^2	0.03	0.04	0.02
D3	MPR	−0.2605(0.1953)	−0.1459(0.1534)	0.1792(0.1763)
	RGDP	−2.91e-12**(1.27e-12)	−3.10e-12***(1.00e-12)	−2.52e-12**(1.15e-12)
	USD	0.5571***(0.1374)	0.4156***(0.1079)	0.3969***(0.1240)
	GFPI	0.0045(0.0080)	0.0144**(0.0063)	0.0109(0.0072)
	Constant	−0.1906***(0.0328)	−0.0096(0.0258)	0.1795***(0.0296)
	Pseudo R^2	0.10	0.10	0.10
D4	MPR	0.0870**(0.0435)	0.1629***(0.0582)	0.1779***(0.0581)
	RGDP	−2.49e-12***(4.25e-13)	−2.25e-12***(5.70e-13)	−2.25e-12***(5.68e-13)
	USD	0.3020***(0.0496)	0.2990***(0.0665)	0.3205***(0.0663)
	GFPI	0.0134***(0.0022)	0.0144***(0.0030)	0.0196***(0.0030)
	Constant	−0.1229***(0.0153)	−0.0127(0.0205)	0.1177***(0.0204)
	Pseudo R^2	0.25	0.26	0.32
S4	MPR	0.1955***(0.0417)	0.1024***(0.0158)	0.0976***(0.0134)
	RGDP	2.98e-12***(7.52e-13)	7.33e-13**(2.85e-13)	5.32e-13**(2.41e-13)
	USD	−0.1934***(0.0501)	−0.0270(0.0190)	0.0145(0.0161)
	GFPI	0.0050(0.0048)	0.0101***(0.0018)	0.0104***(0.0015)
	Constant	−7.5586***(1.942)	−1.9198**(0.7352)	−1.6287**(0.6231)
	Pseudo R^2	0.16	0.35	0.52

Standard errors in parenthesis. *, **, and *** signify 10%, 5% and 1% significance level, respectively.

50th and 75th quantiles, respectively. At the same D4, domestic food prices rise by 0.0134%, 0.0144% and 0.0196% at the 25th, 50th and 75th quantiles respectively following a percentage increase in global food prices.

Turkey

Monetary policy effect on food prices at scale D1 in Turkey is positive but statistically significant only at the 25th quantile (see Table 4.11). A percentage restriction of monetary policy leads to a 0.993% increase in food prices at the 25th quantile. Over the long medium-term horizon (scales D2 and D3), monetary policy effect on food prices in Turkey is

Table 4.11 Results on Turkey

Scales	Variables	25th Quantile	50th Quantile	75th Quantile
D1	MPR	0.9929**(0.4706)	0.5482(0.5104)	0.6720(0.5951)
	RGDP	2.60e-08(6.18e-08)	−2.51e-08(6.71e-08)	−8.52e-08(7.82e-08)
	USD	2.349(3.6928)	5.4450(4.0056)	8.4995*(4.6704)
	GFPI	−0.0045(0.0775)	0.0286(0.0841)	−0.0193(0.0980)
	Constant	−0.7180***(0.1058)	−0.0801(0.1148)	0.8424***(0.1338)
	Pseudo R^2	0.055	0.06	0.07
D2	MPR	0.1549(0.5795)	−0.2176(0.4718)	0.1516(0.5548)
	RGDP	−3.78e-08(5.98e-08)	−4.41e-08(4.87e-08)	−1.02e-07*(5.72e-08)
	USD	4.8370(3.8909)	5.3314*(3.1678)	10.9868***(3.725)
	GFPI	0.1441(0.0896)	0.1014(0.0729)	0.0243(0.0858)
	Constant	−0.9332***(0.1936)	−0.0386(0.1576)	0.9844***(0.1854)
	Pseudo R^2	0.06	0.05	0.04
D3	MPR	−0.0208(0.2773)	0.0601(0.2538)	−0.1622(0.3462)
	RGDP	4.09e-08(3.83e-08)	6.54e-08*(3.51e-08)	6.36e-09(4.78e-08)
	USD	−1.2340(2.6033)	−2.3438(2.3826)	1.0906(3.2498)
	GFPI	0.0419(0.0388)	0.0128(0.0355)	0.0645(0.0484)
	Constant	−0.9113***(0.1507)	−0.1301(0.1379)	0.8320***(0.1881)
	Pseudo R^2	0.05	0.04	0.04
D4	MPR	0.9443**(0.2405)	0.9234***(0.1566)	0.9106***(0.1412)
	RGDP	1.63e-07***(5.05e-08)	1.94e-07***(3.29e-08)	1.60e-07***(2.96e-08)
	USD	−8.6700*(4.4037)	−10.5584***(2.8686)	−6.6864**(2.5862)
	GFPI	−0.0308(0.0397)	−0.0509*(0.0259)	−0.0461*(0.0233)
	Constant	−0.6924***(0.1992)	0.1182(0.1297)	0.8509***(0.1170)
	Pseudo R^2	0.32	0.33	0.33
S4	MPR	0.2673***(0.0442)	0.3368***(0.0637)	0.2888***(0.0427)
	RGDP	4.27e-08***(9.03e-09)	2.92e-08**(1.30e-08)	6.40e-08***(8.72e-09)
	USD	−3.5379***(0.6698)	−1.8413*(0.9660)	−4.0802***(0.6472)
	GFPI	0.0467***(0.0143)	0.0209(0.0206)	0.0032(0.0138)
	Constant	−0.3759(1.9258)	1.4096(2.7773)	−3.5020*(1.8607)
	Pseudo R^2	0.23	0.26	0.41

Standard errors in parenthesis. *, **, and *** signify 10%, 5% and 1% significance level, respectively.

statistically not significant. Over the long-term horizon (scale D4), monetary policy effect on food prices is positive and statistically significant at all the quantiles of food inflation. A percentage monetary policy contraction in Turkey at D4 elicits 0.944%, 0.923% and 0.911% increase in food prices at the 25th, 50th and 75th quantiles, respectively. The long-term trend (S4) also shows that the monetary policy effect on food prices is positive and statistically significant at all the quantiles.

The effect of real gross domestic product on food inflation in Turkey is mixed. At scale D2, real gross domestic product impacts food prices negatively but statistically significant only at the 75th quantile. At scales D3 and D4, real gross domestic product exerts positive effect on food prices in Turkey. At scale D1, the exchange rate of the Turkish Lira to the United States Dollars exerts positive effect on food prices but is statistically significant only at the 75th quantile. Food prices rise by 8.4995% at the 75th quantile following a percentage depreciation of the Lira. At scale D2, a percentage depreciation of the Lira engenders an increase of 5.3314% and 10.9868% in food prices at the median and the 75th quantile, respectively. At scale D4, however, a percentage depreciation of the Lira leads to a decline in food prices by 8.67%, 10.56% and 6.69% at the 25th, 50th and 75th quantiles, respectively. Global food prices exert negative impact on domestic food prices in Turkey at the median and the 75th quantile in scale D4. A percentage rise in global food prices leads to 0.051% and 0.046% fall in domestic food prices at the median and 75th quantile, respectively, in Turkey.

Robustness checks

The resilience of the results is tested by varying the earlier specifications. Real gross domestic product is replaced by real household consumption expenditure and real gross fixed capital formation. The results largely remain robust across the scales and quantiles. For the sake of space, the robustness results are presented in the appendix.

Policy discussion

The descriptive analysis in chapter 3 brought to fore an underlying volatility in food prices in all the countries under study. The analysis also points to the fact food prices largely underlie overall inflation path in these countries. Importantly, the empirical chapter shows that monetary policy exerts positive impact on food prices in most of these countries. These present important policy challenges to the inflation targeting countries. Inflation targeting central banks are in a better position to set and achieve inflation targets when they can reasonably forecast the future path of inflation with considerable accuracy. When the path of overall inflation is intertwined with food price trajectory, as observed in chapter 3, the resulting overall inflation series would necessarily carry the volatile feature of food prices, given the dominance of food in the consumption baskets of many of these developing and emerging countries. As a consequence, an accurate forecast of overall inflation is problematic. If overall inflation does not lend itself to a reasonably accurate forecast, then the achievement of publicly announced inflation target would naturally be in limbo. When inflation targets are missed, the credibility of central banks becomes questionable and anchoring public inflation expectation to the announced target becomes extremely difficult, if not impossible.

Food price increases are said to engender overall inflation hikes requiring monetary policy contraction. Meanwhile, monetary policy tightening destabilises food prices further, a dilemma that often confronts inflation targeting central banks in developing and emerging economies. The dilemma is confounded by the realities of inflation target breaches in countries such as Brazil, Chile, Ghana, Hungary, Mexico, Russia, South Africa and Turkey, where monetary policy contraction positively impacts food prices over different horizons and at distinct quantiles. In Brazil, the upper band of the inflation tolerance range was breached in 2002, 2003, 2011, 2015 and 2016. Chile had a similar experience in 2007, 2008, 2014 and 2015. For Ghana, inflation target was achieved only in 2010, 2011 and 2012 over the period under review. The targets were breached in the remainder of the years over the inflation targeting period in Ghana. Hungary missed the inflation targets from 2001 up to 2004 as well as between 2006 and 2012. Mexico, Russia, South Africa and Turkey have equally had their own challenges of breaching the inflation targets in some of the years over their respective inflation targeting regimes. For these countries with positive monetary policy impact on food prices, Bhattacharya & Jain (2020) prescribe monetary policy contraction on a continuous basis such that the intended negative impact through the channel of aggregate demand would more than offset the positive impact through the channel of production cost. However, as observed by Iddrisu & Alagidede (2020), such a sustained tightening of monetary policy may damage the growth prospects of emerging and developing economies where economic growth is essentially a necessity, given the low income and development levels.

Ginn & Pourroy (2020) postulated that a complementary fiscal policy in the form of food price subsidy is critical to avoid an overly contractionary monetary policy stance. Such a policy prescription, they argue, is ideal for countries where food is a major component of the consumption basket and where households suffer credit constraints. This policy prescription, undoubtedly, fits the developing and emerging countries better. Indeed, given the high poverty levels in these countries and the argument that food prices are ruinous to the poor relative to the rich (Hanif, 2012), then it presents welfare call on fiscal authorities entrusted with the welfare of the citizens. Importantly, the architecture of inflation targeting in these countries provide a significant role for the government to play. In fact, it is the fiscal authorities that set inflation targets or jointly set it with the central banks in many of these countries. Having fiscal policies that shave off these burdens from monetary policy authorities would not be out of place.

For Colombia and Indonesia, the stabilising effect of restrictive monetary policy on food inflation over the short-to-medium-term horizons presents different policy options. Monetary policy does not have to be continuously contractive, and complementary monetary and fiscal policies may not be the exact panacea. In Colombia, because monetary policy stabilises food prices over the two-to-four-month horizon, the monetary policy authorities must have a reasonably ac-curate forecast of the path of food prices and devise an appropriate restrictive policy response. When food prices are expected to take an upturn, a preemptive restrictive monetary policy that exacts sub-stantial negative impact over two-to-four-month horizon would help nip not only food prices in the bud but also potential overall inflation momentum, given the entwined food and overall inflation paths in the country. It would also avoid the possible second-round impact of food prices on overall inflation in Colombia. This is especially so as monetary policy effect on food prices in Colombia over the longer horizons is destabilising. This brings to fore the need for the monetary policy authorities in Colombia to comprehend the dynamics and timing of the transmission of the monetary policy decisions. With such an understanding and knowledge of food price paths (from forecasts), the monetary policy authorities are better positioned to exact the needed stability in food prices over the short horizon in a manner that could potentially avert second-round effect of food prices which may underpin the destabilising effect over the longer horizons. Similar policy dynamics apply to Indonesia where monetary policy restriction provides stability in food prices over the four-to-eight-month and the eight-to-sixteen-month horizons. Monetary policy effect on food prices in Indonesia becomes statistically meaningful from the four-to-eight-month horizon but not the very short horizon of two-to-four-month as observed in Colombia. A forward-looking monetary policy restriction meant to have an impact on rising food prices over the very short horizon like the case of Colombia may then not achieve the intended effect. Monetary policy authorities in Indonesia, just like those in Colombia, would require a comprehension of the transmission channel dynamics and timing to deliver the expected stability in food prices over the right horizons. Getting the timing right and under-standing the future path of food inflation in Indonesia is even more critical, given the fact that food prices in the country appear to define the overall inflation path. As observed in the previous chapter, declines (rises) in overall inflation in Indonesia coincide with periods when food inflation had dropped (risen) significantly. Stabilising food prices over the appropriate horizons then provide some stability in the overall inflation and engender the achievement of the publicly announced inflation targets.

The growing importance of food items such as grains and seeds as inputs for biofuel production makes the findings of this study relevant to the energy sector. The energy sector relies on biofuel as a viable alternative to crude oil in view of the variabilities and the expensive nature of the latter. However, as observed by Iddrisu & Alagidede (2020), the observed food price volatilities, coupled with food price destabilization by monetary policy restriction negate the appeal of biofuels relative to crude oil. Furthermore, agriculture and farming in particular is the mainstay of many folks in emerging and developing economies. The positive monetary policy impact on food prices and the observed food price volatilities holds policy relevance for farmers in these countries. Whiles food price increases occasioned by monetary policy restrictions are good for the incomes of farmers, the underlying volatilities in food prices can swing those incomes to the extremes and inflict unexpected losses. Indeed, such volatilities blight planning efforts of the farmers and ravage output prospects.

References

Aguiar-Conraria, L., Azevedo, N., & Soares, M. J. (2008). Using wavelets to decompose the time–frequency effects of monetary policy. *Physica A: Statistical Mechanics and its Applications, 387*(12), 2863–2878.

Akram, Q. F. (2009). Commodity prices, interest rates and the dollar. *Energy Economics 31*, 838–851.

Alper, C. E., Hobdari, N., & Uppal, A. (2016). Food inflation in Sub-Saharan Africa: Causes and policy implications. *IMF Working Paper*. WP/16/247.

Anand, R., & Prasad, E. S. (2010). Optimal price indices for targeting inflation under incomplete markets. *Working Paper 16290, National Bureau of Economic Research.*

Anand, R., Prasad, E. S., & Zhang, B. (2015). What measure of inflation should a developing country central bank target? *Journal of Monetary Economics 74*, 102–116.

Anzuini, A., Lombardi, M. J., & Pagano, P. (2010) The impact of monetary policy shocks on commodity prices. *European Central Bank Working Paper Series No. 1232/August 2010*, 1–27.

Aoki, K. (2001). Optimal monetary policy responses to relative-price changes. *Journal of Monetary Economics, 48*, 55–80.

Bhattacharya, R., & Jain, R. (2020). Can monetary policy stabilise food inflation? Evidence from advanced and emerging economies. *Economic Modelling, 89*, 122–141.

Catao, L. A., & Chang, R. (2015). World food prices and monetary policy. *Journal of Monetary Economics, 75*, 69–88.

Crowley, P. M. (2007). A guide to wavelets for economists. *Journal of Economic Surveys, 21*(2), 207–267.

Daubechies, I. (1992). *Ten lectures on wavelets* (Vol. 61). Siam.

De Gregorio, J. (2012). Commodity prices, monetary policy and inflation. *Serie Documentos De Trabajo. SDT, 359.*

Frankel, J. A. (2008). The effect of monetary policy on real commodity prices. *A Book Chapter in the Volume: Asset Prices and Monetary Policy.* University of Chicago Press, p. 291–333.

Ginn, W., & Pourroy, M. (2020). Should a central bank react to food inflation? Evidence from an estimated model for Chile. *Economic Modelling, 90*, 221–234.

Gómez, M. I., González, E. R., & Melo, L. F. (2012). Forecasting food inflation in developing countries with inflation targeting regimes. *American Journal of Agricultural Economics, 94*(1), 153–173.

Hammoudeh, S., Nguyen, D. K., & Sousa, R. M. (2015). US monetary policy and sectoral commodity prices. *Journal of International Money and Finance 57*, 61–85.

Hanif, M. N. (2012). A note on food inflation in Pakistan. *Pakistan Economic and Social Review, 50*(2), 183–206.

Iddrisu, A. A., & Alagidede, I. P. (2020). Monetary policy and food inflation in South Africa: A quantile regression analysis. *Food Policy*, 101816.

Iddrisu A. A., & Alagidede, I. P. (2021). Asymmetry in food price responses to monetary policy: A quantile regression approach. *SN Business and Economics, 1*, 52.

Mensi, W., Hammoudeh, S., & Tiwari, A. K. (2016). New evidence on hedges and safe havens for Gulf stock markets using the wavelet-based quantile. *Emerging Markets Review, 28*, 155–183.

Pourroy, M., Carton, B., & Coulibaly, D. (2016). Food prices and inflation targeting in emerging economies. *International Economics, 146*, 108–140.

Sargent, T. J., & Wallace, N. (1981). Some unpleasant monetarist arithmetic. Federal Reserve Bank of Minneapolis. *Quarterly Review.* Fall issue.

Scrimgeour, D. (2014). Commodity price responses to monetary policy surprises. *American Journal of Agricultural Economics, 97*(1), 88–102.

Šoškić, D. (2015). Inflation impact of food prices: Case of Serbia. *Economics of Agriculture*, 1/2015 UDC: 338.516.49:336.748.12:338.439.4(497.11).

Tiwari, A. K., Dar, A. B., & Bhanja, N. (2013). Oil price and exchange rates: A wavelet based analysis for India. *Economic Modelling, 31*, 414–422.

Wagan, Z. A., Chen, Z., Seelro, H., & Shah, M. S. (2018). Assessing the effect of monetary policy on agricultural growth and food prices. *Agric. Econ. – Czech*, *64*(11), 499–507.

Walsh, J. (2011). Reconsidering the role of food prices in inflation. *IMF Working Paper*, WP11/71.

Yang, L., Tian, S., Yang, W., Xu, M., & Hamori, S. (2018). Dependence structures between Chinese stock markets and the international financial market: Evidence from a wavelet-based quantile regression approach. *The North American Journal of Economics and Finance*, *45*, 116–137.

Appendix

Table 4.12 Robustness results for Brazil

Scales	Variables	25th Quantile	50th Quantile	75th Quantile
D1	MPR	−0.074(0.188)	−0.281(0.184)	−0.165(0.152)
	HCE	−7.47e-06(0.00002)	−0.00004**(0.00002)	−0.0000264*(0.0000-15)
	GFCF	−0.00014(0.0001)	0.00002(0.00009)	0.00001(0.00007)
	USD	−0.718(0.851)	−0.250(0.831)	−0.1445(0.689)
	GFPI	−0.0096(0.0187)	−0.029(0.018)	0.00001(0.016)
	Constant	−0.147***(0.0249)	0.0123(0.0243)	0.155***(0.020)
	Pseudo R^2	0.10	0.10	0.10
D2	MPR	−0.450(0.480)	0.147(0.540)	−0.538(0.413)
	HCE	−0.00005(0.00004)	−3.65e-06(0.00004)	−0.00005(0.00003)
	GFCF	−0.00003(0.00009)	−0.00016(0.0001)	5.23e-06(0.00008)
	USD	−0.924(1.064)	0.093(1.198)	−1.688*(0.917)
	GFPI	−0.0095(0.027)	−0.013(0.030)	−0.059**(0.023)
	Constant	−0.390***(0.055)	0.0197(0.0614)	0.328***(0.047)
	Pseudo R^2	0.10	0.10	0.10
D3	MPR	0.372(0.334)	−0.073(0.330)	0.318(0.432)
	HCE	0.00002(0.00003)	−0.00001(0.00003)	0.000015(0.000042)
	GFCF	0.0001(0.0001)	0.00011(0.0001)	0.00003(0.0001)
	USD	0.924(1.022)	−0.2175(1.010)	−0.442(1.322)
	GFPI	0.0001(0.0194)	−0.0106(0.019)	0.0302(0.0251)
	Constant	−0.530***(0.073)	−0.094(0.072)	0.4503***(0.0944)
	Pseudo R^2	0.04	0.02	0.04
D4	MPR	1.208***(0.201)	1.426***(0.172)	1.678***(0.275)
	HCE	0.00004**(0.00002)	0.00007***(0.00002)	0.00009***(0.00003)
	GFCF	0.00002(0.00005)	0.00005(0.000045)	−0.00008(0.00007)
	USD	4.2266***(1.072)	3.950***(0.918)	4.0854***(1.4699)
	GFPI	0.0974***(0.0220)	0.0915***(0.0189)	0.1248***(0.030)
	Constant	−0.806***(0.115)	−0.0628(0.0988)	0.6116***(0.1582)
	Pseudo R^2	0.34	0.35	0.30
S4	MPR	0.028(0.202)	−0.0297(0.3917)	−0.142(0.249)
	HCE	−0.0001***(0.00002)	−0.00011***(0.00004)	−0.0001***(0.00002)
	GFCF	0.0004***(0.00003)	0.0003***(0.0001)	0.00024***(0.00004)
	USD	14.916***(1.751)	11.152***(3.399)	11.104***(2.162)
	GFPI	0.221***(0.0242)	0.1039**(0.0469)	0.0798***(0.0298)
	Constant	−27.245***(4.398)	−6.315(8.535)	14.446***(5.428)
	Pseudo R^2	0.50	0.28	0.29

Standard errors in parenthesis. *, **, and *** signify 10%, 5% and 1% significance level, respectively.

Table 4.13 Robustness results for Chile

Scales	Variables	25th Quantile	50th Quantile	75th Quantile
D1	MPR	0.8671(0.5405)	0.6416(0.4952)	0.5113(0.4318)
	HCE	−1.63e-07(4.03e-07)	−3.05e-07(3.69e-07)	−1.10e-07(3.22e-07)
	GFCF	1.48e-07(1.37e-06)	2.11e-08(1.25e-06)	−6.84e-07(1.09e-06)
	USD	0.0166**(0.0076)	0.0088(0.0070)	0.0134**(0.0061)
	GFPI	0.0666**(0.0281)	0.0637**(0.02257)	0.0862***(0.0224)
	Constant	−0.1969***(0.0360)	0.0081(0.0330)	0.1928***(0.0288)
	Pseudo R^2	0.10	0.10	0.13
D2	MPR	0.4873(0.4299)	0.7222**(0.3364)	0.4628(0.5238)
	HCE	−8.23e-07**(3.54e-07)	−6.66e-07**(2.77e-07)	−5.03e-07(4.32e-07)
	GFCF	1.55e-06(1.16e-06)	1.56e-06(9.06e-07)	1.27e-06(1.41e-06)
	USD	0.0237**(0.0104)	0.0170**(0.0082)	0.0153(0.0127)
	GFPI	0.0423(0.0371)	0.0721**(0.0290)	0.1270***(0.0452)
	Constant	−0.3855***(0.0721)	−0.0970*(0.0564)	0.3895***(0.0878)
	Pseudo R^2	0.11	0.10	0.10
D3	MPR	−0.1362(0.3632)	−0.3111(0.3256)	−0.2448(0.2946)
	HCE	−7.42e-07**(3.75e-07)	−8.16e-07**(3.36e-07)	−3.74e-07(3.04e-07)
	GFCF	1.47e-06(1.08e-06)	1.16e-06(9.72e-07)	−1.66e-07(8.79e-07)
	USD	0.0156(0.0163)	0.0097(0.0146)	0.0272**(0.0133)
	GFPI	0.0278(0.0390)	−0.0330(0.0350)	0.0241(0.0317)
	Constant	−0.6267***(0.1150)	0.0487(0.1031)	0.5541***(0.0933)
	Pseudo R^2	0.03	0.04	0.055
D4	MPR	1.5666***(0.3703)	1.5377***(0.3019)	1.7841***(0.2994)
	HCE	8.21e-07(6.22e-07)	9.58e-07*(5.07e-07)	1.88e-06***(5.03e-07)
	GFCF	3.11e-07(1.58e-06)	−7.28e-07(1.29e-06)	−3.26e-06**(1.28e-06)
	USD	−0.0327(0.0234)	−0.0675***(0.0191)	−0.0691***(0.0189)
	GFPI	−0.0368(0.0472)	−0.1017**(0.0385)	−0.0766**(0.0381)
	Constant	−0.8421***(0.1801)	0.1212(0.1469)	0.9948***(0.1456)
	Pseudo R^2	0.29	0.24	0.27
S4	MPR	0.7289***(0.2782)	1.5314***(0.2898)	1.6905***(0.1229)
	HCE	−1.71e-06***(4.02e-07)	−2.62e-06***(4.19e-07)	−2.44e-06***(1.78e-07)
	GFCF	4.79e-06***(1.04e-06)	6.29e-06***(1.09e-06)	6.23e-06***(4.60e-07)
	USD	0.0182**(0.0071)	0.0383***(0.0074)	0.0450***(0.0031)
	GFPI	0.1019***(0.0337)	0.0957***(0.0351)	0.1136***(0.0149)
	Constant	−10.9230***(3.8362)	−16.1427***(3.9960)	−22.3597***(1.6949)
	Pseudo R^2	0.38	0.47	0.63

Standard errors in parenthesis. *, **, and *** signify 10%, 5% and 1% significance level, respectively.

Table 4.14 Robustness results for Colombia

Scales	Variables	25th Quantile	50th Quantile	75th Quantile
D1	MPR	−0.3118(0.4015)	−0.3035(0.2562)	−0.7851**(0.3498)
	HCE	1.04e-07(1.61e-07)	1.60e-07(1.03e-07)	1.63e-08(1.41e-07)
	GFCF	−7.75e-07(5.09e-07)	−9.72e-07***(3.25e-07)	−5.42e-07(4.43e-07)
	USD	−0.0080(0.0115)	−0.0075(0.0073)	−0.0058(0.0100)
	GFPI	0.0324(0.0332)	0.0177(0.0212)	−0.0125(0.0289)
	Constant	−0.2037***(0.0444)	−0.0004(0.0283)	0.1858***(0.0386)
	Pseudo R^2	0.15	0.12	0.13
D2	MPR	2.3191***(0.7864)	1.4976*(0.8237)	0.6799(0.9704)
	HCE	2.15e-09(9.88e-08)	1.78e-07*(1.03e-07)	1.19e-07(1.22e-07)
	GFCF	−1.75e-07(2.82e-07)	−7.03e-07**(2.95e-07)	−6.62e-07*(3.48e-07)
	USD	−0.0075(0.0113)	−0.0094(0.0118)	−0.0011(0.0139)
	GFPI	−0.0705**(0.0309)	−0.0393(0.0324)	−0.0387(0.0382)
	Constant	−0.4909***(0.0636)	−0.0400(0.0666)	0.3392***(0.0784)
	Pseudo R^2	0.13	0.10	0.11
D3	MPR	1.5771***(0.5626)	1.1212***(0.3496)	1.3496**(0.5594)
	HCE	2.04e-07*(1.19e-07)	1.65e-07**(7.42e-08)	2.21e-07*(1.19e-07)
	GFCF	−9.71e-07**(4.06e-07)	−8.70e-07***(2.52e-07)	−9.09e-07**(4.04e-07)
	USD	−0.0028(0.0125)	−0.0031(0.0078)	−0.0123(0.0125)
	GFPI	−0.0684**(0.0301)	−0.0791***(0.0187)	−0.0739**(0.0299)
	Constant	−0.4675***(0.1049)	−0.0766(0.0652)	0.5190***(0.1043)
	Pseudo R^2	0.21	0.24	0.21
D4	MPR	2.5461***(0.3577)	2.2803***(0.2045)	2.2331***(0.3957)
	HCE	5.72e-08(1.29e-07)	3.52e-07***(7.38e-08)	4.12e-07***(1.43e-07)
	GFCF	−3.46e-07(3.81e-07)	−1.16e-06***(2.18e-07)	−1.28e-06***(4.22e-07)
	USD	0.0002(0.0288)	0.0139(0.0165)	0.0117(0.03183)
	GFPI	−0.0599*(0.0310)	−0.0451**(0.0177)	−0.0162(0.0343)
	Constant	−0.6916***(0.1683)	−0.0011(0.0962)	0.8381***(0.1861)
	Pseudo R^2	0.31	0.31	0.34
S4	MPR	2.0113***(0.0831)	1.9560***(0.1899)	1.9197***(0.1521)
	HCE	−2.21e-07***(3.69e-08)	−3.07e-07***(8.43e-08)	−4.43e-07***(6.76e-08)
	GFCF	8.65e-07***(1.22e-07)	1.25e-06***(2.79e-07)	1.93e-06***(2.23e-07)
	USD	−0.0288***(0.0047)	−0.0156(0.0107)	−0.0049(0.0085)
	GFPI	−0.0844***(0.0126)	−0.0695**(0.0287)	−0.0250(0.0230)
	Constant	−12.0149(1.4502)	−15.6711(3.3135)	−23.4849***(2.6542)
	Pseudo R^2	0.59	0.57	0.63

Standard errors in parenthesis. *, **, and *** signify 10%, 5% and 1% significance level, respectively.

Table 4.15 Robustness results for Ghana

Scales	Variables	25th Quantile	50th Quantile	75th Quantile
D1	MPR	−0.0399(0.2316)	−0.0330(0.1506)	−0.3737(0.2316)
	HCE	−1.88e-10(1.14e-10)	−1.12e-10(7.40e-11)	−2.02e-10*(1.14e-10)
	GFCF	4.53e-10(7.85e-10)	2.90e-10(5.10e-10)	9.97e-10(7.85e-10)
	USD	0.7530(1.4617)	−0.0890(0.9505)	0.8843(1.4616)
	GFPI	0.0440(0.0397)	0.0056(0.0258)	0.0847**(0.0397)
	Constant	−0.2140***(0.0530)	−0.0164(0.0344)	0.2114***(0.0530
	Pseudo R^2	0.06	0.06	0.10
D2	MPR	−0.1917(0.3079)	0.0945(0.1849)	0.2829(0.2908)
	HCE	1.27e-11(1.17e-10)	1.51e-11(7.03e-11)	−1.03e-10(1.11e-10)
	GFCF	−4.30e-10(4.37e-10)	−6.71e-10**(2.62e-10)	−8.33e-10**(4.12e-10)
	USD	−0.1881(1.8669)	−0.2183(1.1210)	1.4881(1.7629)
	GFPI	−0.0334(0.03160)	−0.0213(0.0190)	−0.0473(0.0298)
	Constant	−0.3263***(0.0686)	0.00009(0.0412)	0.3293***(0.0648)
	Pseudo R^2	0.06	0.06	0.07
D3	MPR	0.5006*(0.2896)	0.3222(0.2370)	0.7174**(0.3101)
	HCE	2.39e-11(1.12e-10)	−7.74e-11(9.20e-11)	−1.31e-10(1.20e-10)
	GFCF	6.52e-10*(3.36e-10)	−7.19e-11(2.75e-10)	−4.01e-10(3.60e-10)
	USD	−3.5790**(1.6776)	−0.2348(1.3728)	0.7335(1.7964)
	GFPI	0.0175(0.0235)	0.0434**(0.0193)	0.0419*(0.0252)
	Constant	−0.5582***(0.0913)	0.0438(0.0747)	0.5499***(0.0978)
	Pseudo R^2	0.14	0.12	0.14
D4	MPR	0.5014***(0.1601)	0.4007***(0.1207)	0.6926***(0.1410)
	HCE	−6.80e-11(5.27e-11)	−2.86e-11(3.97e-11)	1.06e-10**(4.64e-11)
	GFCF	6.53e-10***(1.09e-10)	5.15e-10***(8.22e-11)	3.22e-10***(9.60e-11)
	USD	−0.4820(0.8666)	−1.2231*(0.6532)	−3.4665***(0.7632)
	GFPI	−0.0199**(0.0083)	−0.0334***(0.0062)	−0.0363***(0.0073)
	Constant	−0.3369***(0.0728)	0.0121(0.0549)	0.3733***(0.0641)
	Pseudo R^2	0.43	0.46	0.47
S4	MPR	0.7126***(0.0776)	1.2617***(0.1964)	1.1297***(0.1941)
	HCE	−8.38e-11***(2.04e-11)	−1.28e-10**(5.15e-11)	−1.34e-10**(5.09e-11)
	GFCF	6.15e-11**(2.65e-11)	1.12e-12(6.71e-11)	−1.90e-10***(6.63e-11)
	USD	−3.127***(0.4006)	−4.2477***(1.0138)	−2.1882**(1.0020)
	GFPI	−0.0400***(0.0129)	−0.0643**(0.0326)	−0.0381(0.0322)
	Constant	7.2939***(2.1017)	6.7333(5.3186)	11.4414**(5.2568)
	Pseudo R^2	0.39	0.33	0.47

Standard errors in parenthesis. *, **, and *** signify 10%, 5% and 1% significance level, respectively.

Table 4.16 Robustness results for Hungary

Scales	Variables	25th Quantile	50th Quantile	75th Quantile
D1	MPR	0.4710(0.3458)	0.3394(0.3267)	0.0098(0.3774)
	HCE	4.26e-06(4.85e-06)	4.48e-06(4.59e-06)	−8.87e-07(5.30e-06)
	GFCF	6.10e-06*(3.41e-06)	6.60e-06**(3.22e-06)	5.39e-06(3.72e-06)
	USD	−0.01464(0.0120)	−0.0236**(0.0113)	−0.0193(0.0131)
	GFPI	0.0304(0.0271)	0.0493*(0.0256)	0.0195(0.0296)
	Constant	−0.2085***(0.0337)	0.0171(0.0256)	0.1855***(0.0401)
	Pseudo R^2	0.04	0.06	0.04
D2	MPR	0.2634(0.3595)	0.6108**(0.2739)	0.5040(0.3232)
	HCE	6.87e-06*(3.66e-06)	7.19e-06**(2.79e-06)	6.09e-06*(3.29e-06)
	GFCF	1.51e-06(2.86e-06)	4.87e-06**(2.18e-06)	4.93e-06*(2.57e-06)
	USD	−0.0138(0.0179)	−0.0227*(0.0136)	−0.0190(0.0161)
	GFPI	0.1123***(0.0345)	0.0849***(0.0263)	0.0722**(0.0310)
	Constant	−0.3342***(0.0671)	−0.0089(0.0512)	0.3146***(0.0604)
	Pseudo R^2	0.12	0.11	0.12
D3	MPR	0.4006(0.3941)	0.9878**(0.4852)	1.6796***(0.4678)
	HCE	7.93e-06**(2.77e-06)	0.000012***(3.42e-06)	0.000013***(3.29e-06)
	GFCF	2.02e-06(2.55e-06)	4.80e-06(3.14e-06)	3.31e-06(3.03e-06)
	USD	0.0267(0.0174)	0.0286(0.0215)	0.0665***(0.0207)
	GFPI	0.1369***(0.0258)	0.1217***(0.0317)	0.1782***(0.0306)
	Constant	−0.6123***(0.0818)	−0.0287(0.1007)	0.5545***(0.0971)
	Pseudo R^2	0.20	0.14	0.20
D4	MPR	1.5354***(0.4069)	1.6790***(0.4974)	0.8229**(0.3913)
	HCE	6.96e-06(4.98e-06)	3.95e-06(6.09e-06)	−5.64e-06(4.79e-06)
	GFCF	8.20e-06**(3.97e-06)	0.000011**(4.85e-06)	8.43e-06**(3.82e-06)
	USD	0.0220(0.0254)	0.0392(0.0310)	−0.0246(0.0244)
	GFPI	0.1262***(0.0295)	0.1628***(0.0361)	0.1155***(0.0284)
	Constant	−1.0864***(0.1456)	0.0034(0.1779)	0.9162***(0.1400)
	Pseudo R^2	0.13	0.14	0.24
S4	MPR	0.4790**(0.2317)	1.2835***(0.2742)	1.8558***(0.0796)
	HCE	0.000022***(3.09e-06)	9.81e-06**(3.66e-06)	4.00e-06***(1.06e-06)
	GFCF	−0.000011***(2.29e-06)	−1.54e-06(2.71e-06)	5.57e-06***(7.85e-07)
	USD	−0.0703***(0.0228)	0.0189(0.0269)	0.0424***(0.0078)
	GFPI	0.0676**(0.0289)	0.1481***(0.0342)	0.1419***(0.0099)
	Constant	−47.8813***(6.7152)	−40.8709***(7.9453)	−36.9807***(2.3053)
	Pseudo R^2	0.64	0.69	0.77

Standard errors in parenthesis. *, **, and *** signify 10%, 5% and 1% significance level, respectively.

Table 4.17 Robustness results for Indonesia

Scales	Variables	25th Quantile	50th Quantile	75th Quantile
D1	MPR	0.7987(1.1040)	0.4715(1.1917)	0.8671(1.2074)
	HCE	−1.27e-08(3.02e-08)	−5.22e-08(3.26e-08)	3.88e-08(3.30e-08)
	GFCF	1.87e-08(4.38e-08)	6.83e-08(4.73e-08)	−5.52e-08(4.79e-08)
	USD	−0.0073(0.0063)	−0.0038(0.0068)	−0.0043(0.0069)
	GFPI	−0.0224(0.0451)	−0.0439(0.0487)	−0.0343(0.0493)
	Constant	−0.4227***(0.0599)	−0.0046(0.0647)	0.3964***(0.0655)
	Pseudo R^2	0.04	0.06	0.06
D2	MPR	2.4124*(1.3920)	2.8228**(1.4036)	2.2924*(1.3263)
	HCE	3.13e-08(2.38e-08)	1.42e-08(2.40e-08)	1.67e-08(2.27e-08)
	GFCF	−8.29e-09(3.64e-08)	2.46e-08(3.67e-08)	8.29e-09(3.47e-08)
	USD	0.0311***(0.0112)	0.0214*(0.0113)	0.0193*(0.0107)
	GFPI	−0.0372(0.0545)	−0.0431(0.0550)	−0.0693(0.0520)
	Constant	−0.5734***(0.1129)	−0.1028(0.1138)	0.6903***(0.1075)
	Pseudo R^2	0.065	0.08	0.05
D3	MPR	−0.0915(0.2131)	−0.5639**(0.2510)	−0.8614***(0.2382)
	HCE	1.20e-08*(6.96e-09)	8.02e-09(8.20e-09)	8.53e-09(7.78e-09)
	GFCF	−1.74e-08*(9.96e-09)	−2.09e-08*(1.17e-08)	−2.63e-08**(1.11e-08)
	USD	0.0180***(0.0036)	0.0142***(0.0042)	0.0115***(0.0040)
	GFPI	−0.0494***(0.0105)	−0.0480***(0.0124)	−0.0549***(0.0117)
	Constant	−0.2575***(0.0390)	0.0205(0.0460)	0.2563***(0.0436)
	Pseudo R^2	0.15	0.14	0.17
D4	MPR	0.1345(0.1182)	0.0667(0.1142)	0.0555(0.0844)
	HCE	−3.01e-10(4.99e-09)	−4.31e-09(4.83e-09)	2.09e-09(3.56e-09)
	GFCF	3.99e-09(5.41e-09)	8.93e-09*(5.23e-09)	−6.55e-11(3.86e-09)
	USD	0.0078***(0.0019)	0.0058***(0.0018)	0.0087***(0.0013)
	GFPI	0.0030(0.0039)	0.0108***(0.0038)	0.0077***(0.0028)
	Constant	−0.1909***(0.0287)	−0.0157(0.0278)	0.1723***(0.0205)
	Pseudo R^2	0.28	0.25	0.29
S4	MPR	0.1816***(0.0365)	0.1709***(0.0160)	0.1449***(0.0125)
	HCE	−3.57e-09***(1.01e-09)	−4.41e-09***(4.40e-10)	−4.77e-09***(3.43e-10)
	GFCF	6.69e-09***(1.84e-09)	8.03e-09***(8.03e-10)	8.34e-09***(6.27e-10)
	USD	0.0039***(0.0013)	0.0056***(0.0006)	0.0060***(0.0004)
	GFPI	0.0110***(0.0029)	0.0149***(0.0013)	0.0148***(0.00099)
	Constant	−1.1637**(0.5501)	−0.9868***(0.2406)	−0.5640***(0.1878)
	Pseudo R^2	0.48	0.57	0.65

Standard errors in parenthesis. *, **, and *** signify 10%, 5% and 1% significance level, respectively.

Table 4.18 Robustness results for Mexico

Scales	Variables	25th Quantile	50th Quantile	75th Quantile
D1	MPR	0.2732(1.1178)	0.4008(0.9145)	1.2338(1.0072)
	HCE	−0.000027*(0.000015)	−0.000022*(0.000012)	−0.000034**(0.000013)
	GFCF	0.000029(0.000027)	0.000024(0.000022)	0.000036(0.000024)
	USD	0.2791(0.4240)	0.1894(0.3469)	0.4327(0.3821)
	GFPI	−0.0124(0.0457)	−0.0076(0.0374)	−0.0242(0.0412)
	Constant	−0.3033***(0.0592)	−0.0199(0.0484)	0.2539***(0.0534)
	Pseudo R^2	0.04	0.05	0.08
D2	MPR	0.1287(0.8231)	−0.8346(0.7977)	−1.0745(0.8780)
	HCE	−8.38e-06(5.86e-06)	−6.50e-06(5.68e-06)	−0.000013**(6.25e-06)
	GFCF	0.000019*(0.000010)	0.000017*(0.00001)	0.000016(0.000011)
	USD	−0.0541(0.2455)	−0.2608(0.2379)	−0.0158(0.2618)
	GFPI	−0.0307(0.0268)	−0.0564**(0.0259)	−0.0438(0.0285)
	Constant	−0.3041***(0.0541)	−0.0493(0.0524)	0.3739***(0.0577)
	Pseudo R^2	0.07	0.06	0.07
D3	MPR	−0.4540(0.2769)	0.1250(0.2619)	0.01559(0.3705)
	HCE	−4.66e-06(3.34e-06)	−6.38e-06**(3.16e-06)	−7.60e-06*(4.47e-06)
	GFCF	6.06e-06(6.18e-06)	0.000013**(5.85e-06)	8.65e-06(8.27e-06)
	USD	0.3400***(0.1213)	0.0837(0.1148)	0.3360**(0.1624)
	GFPI	0.0227**(0.0114)	0.0070(0.0108)	−0.0027(0.0152)
	Constant	−0.3072***(0.0447)	−0.0128(0.0423)	0.3012***(0.0598)
	Pseudo R^2	0.08	0.04	0.04
D4	MPR	0.3256***(0.1079)	0.3383***(0.0798)	0.2776***(0.0702)
	HCE	−3.61e-06***(1.29e-06)	−2.95e-06***(9.54e-07)	−1.52e-06*(8.40e-07)
	GFCF	5.38e-06**(2.50e-06)	1.33e-06(1.85e-06)	−1.21e-06(1.63e-06)
	USD	0.0350(0.0764)	0.0851(0.0565)	−0.0117(0.0497)
	GFPI	0.00025(0.0044)	0.0047(0.0033)	−0.00035(0.0029)
	Constant	−0.1226***(0.0257)	0.0083(0.0190)	0.1232***(0.0167)
	Pseudo R^2	0.09	0.15	0.15
S4	MPR	0.0471***(0.0095)	0.0679***(0.0095)	0.0682***(0.0065)
	HCE	−1.16e-06***(1.94e-07)	−9.90e-07***(1.94e-07)	−5.80e-07***(1.33e-07)
	GFCF	5.32e-06***(5.72e-07)	4.79e-06***(5.70e-07)	4.17e-06***(3.91e-07)
	USD	−0.0766***(0.01198)	−0.0610***(0.01195)	−0.0595***(0.0082)
	GFPI	0.00003(0.0013)	−0.0017(0.0013)	−0.0040***(0.0009)
	Constant	−0.2715(0.2808)	−0.5088*(0.2801)	−0.9077***(0.1917)
	Pseudo R^2	0.40	0.46	0.53

Standard errors in parenthesis. *, **, and *** signify 10%, 5% and 1% significance level, respectively.

Table 4.19 Robustness results for Russia

Scales	Variables	25th Quantile	50th Quantile	75th Quantile
D1	MPR	0.0039(0.1053)	0.0582(0.0910)	−0.1743(0.1066)
	HCE	−0.000012***(2.12e-06)	0.000012***(1.83e-06)	−0.000012***(2.15e-06)
	GFCF	0.000015***(4.14e-06)	0.000013***(3.58e-06)	0.000012***(4.20e-06)
	USD	−0.05630(0.0484)	0.0243(0.0418)	0.0225(0.0490)
	GFPI	−0.0056(0.0218)	0.0109(0.0189)	0.0099(0.0221)
	Constant	−0.1987***(0.0300)	−0.0097(0.0259)	0.1713***(0.0304)
	Pseudo R^2	0.25	0.22	0.25
D2	MPR	0.1816(0.1736)	0.0993(0.1478)	0.0467(0.1965)
	HCE	0.000012***(1.98e-06)	−0.000013***(1.68e-06)	−0.00002***(2.24e-06)
	GFCF	0.000012**(4.28e-06)	0.000011***(3.65e-06)	0.00002***(4.85e-06)
	USD	−0.0263(0.0511)	0.0506(0.0435)	0.0349(0.0578)
	GFPI	0.0297(0.0308)	0.0296(0.0262)	0.0222(0.0348)
	Constant	−0.3891***(0.0656)	−0.0208(0.0559)	0.4691***(0.0743)
	Pseudo R^2	0.27	0.23	0.26
D3	MPR	0.5895***(0.1547)	0.7726***(0.1871)	0.8299***(0.2093)
	HCE	−9.18e-06***(1.87e-06)	−3.26e-06(2.26e-06)	−2.02e-06(2.53e-06)
	GFCF	6.44e-06*(3.66e-06)	−2.04e-06(4.43e-06)	−1.35e-06(4.95e-06)
	USD	0.0768(0.0533)	0.0035(0.0644)	−0.0415(0.0720)
	GFPI	0.0914***(0.0207)	0.1143***(0.0251)	0.1007***(0.0280)
	Constant	−0.6193***(0.0885)	0.00025(0.1070)	0.6483***(0.1197)
	Pseudo R^2	0.33	0.29	0.30
D4	MPR	2.2125***(0.3542)	1.4559***(0.3214)	1.7479***(0.2975)
	HCE	−3.83e-06(5.84e-06)	−0.000015***(5.30e-06)	−0.00002***(4.90e-06)
	GFCF	3.15e-06(8.80e-06)	0.000017**(7.99e-06)	0.00003***(7.39e-06)
	USD	−0.1267(0.1485)	0.1821(0.1347)	0.1696(0.1247)
	GFPI	0.0664(0.0548)	0.0473(0.0497)	−0.0252(0.0460)
	Constant	−1.8834***(0.2931)	0.3166(0.2660)	1.3860***(0.2462)
	Pseudo R^2	0.25	0.33	0.40
S4	MPR	3.8414***(0.2216)	3.8835***(0.2577)	3.7970***(0.2168)
	HCE	0.000019***(2.32e-06)	0.000016***(2.70e-06)	0.000013***(2.27e-06)
	GFCF	−0.000013***(3.67e-06)	−9.90e-06***(4.27e-06)	−6.10e-06*(3.59e-06)
	USD	−0.4316***(0.0322)	−0.3582***(0.0374)	−0.3041***(0.0315)
	GFPI	0.2447***(0.0389)	0.2540***(0.0453)	0.2604***(0.0381)
	Constant	−104.97***(8.2132)	−93.607***(9.5499)	−83.156***(8.0357)
	Pseudo R^2	0.50	0.55	0.65

Standard errors in parenthesis. *, **, and *** signify 10%, 5% and 1% significance level, respectively.

Table 4.20 Robustness results for South Africa

Scales	Variables	25th Quantile	50th Quantile	75th Quantile
D1	MPR	−0.3404(0.4418)	−0.2038(0.3485)	−0.0050(0.4952)
	HCE	4.95e-12(1.11e-11)	7.36e-12(8.77e-12)	1.65e-11(1.25e-11)
	GFCF	−1.94e-11(3.03e-11)	−2.48e-11(2.39e-11)	−4.00e-11(3.40e-11)
	USD	−0.2124(0.3087)	−0.1548(0.2436)	−0.3519(0.3461)
	GFPI	−0.0178(0.0331)	−0.0072(0.0261)	0.0023(0.0371)
	Constant	−0.2212***(0.0449)	−0.0034(0.0354)	0.2018***(0.0503)
	Pseudo R^2	0.02	0.03	0.02
D2	MPR	0.5455(0.3796)	0.7296**(0.2720)	0.3239(0.4274)
	HCE	−2.67e-12(3.87e-12)	−2.01e-12(2.77e-12)	4.40e-13(4.36e-12)
	GFCF	5.60e-12(9.29e-12)	8.09e-12(6.66e-12)	−8.78e-13(1.05e-11)
	USD	−0.0210(0.1386)	−0.0503(0.0993)	−0.0857(0.1561)
	GFPI	0.0085(0.0135)	0.0012(0.0097)	0.0068(0.0152)
	Constant	−0.1610***(0.0287)	−0.0219(0.0206)	0.1612***(0.0324)
	Pseudo R^2	0.03	0.05	0.02
D3	MPR	−0.5527***(0.1675)	−0.1659(0.1494)	−0.2183(0.1967)
	HCE	−1.07e-11***(2.57e-12)	−7.79e-12***(2.29e-12)	−9.98e-12***(3.02e-12)
	GFCF	1.70e-11**(6.58e-12)	1.02e-11*(5.87e-12)	1.63e-11**(7.72e-12)
	USD	0.6071***(0.1128)	0.3895***(0.1006)	0.4389***(0.1325)
	GFPI	0.0225***(0.0066)	0.0128**(0.0059)	0.0216**(0.0077)
	Constant	−0.1832***(0.0261)	−0.0073(0.0233)	0.1380***(0.0307)
	Pseudo R^2	0.15	0.13	0.10
D4	MPR	0.0332(0.0544)	−0.0445(0.0493)	−0.0889*(0.0474)
	HCE	−8.54e-12***(1.33e-12)	−1.01e-11***(1.21e-12)	−1.00e-11***(1.16e-12)
	GFCF	1.26e-11***(3.10e-12)	1.64e-11***(2.81e-12)	1.66e-11***(2.71e-12)
	USD	0.3175***(0.0544)	0.3755***(0.0494)	0.3928***(0.0475)
	GFPI	0.0214***(0.0031)	0.0274***(0.0028)	0.0315***(0.0027)
	Constant	−0.0793***(0.0161)	−0.0068(0.0146)	0.1066***(0.0141)
	Pseudo R^2	0.30	0.36	0.43
S4	MPR	0.1731***(0.0366)	0.1050***(0.0258)	0.1021***(0.0177)
	HCE	3.16e-12***((1.13e-12)	1.06e-12(7.96e-13)	8.72e-13(5.46e-13)
	GFCF	2.97e-12(1.87e-12)	8.12e-13(1.32e-12)	1.67e-13(9.04e-13)
	USD	−0.1631***(0.0336)	−0.0305(0.0237)	0.0110(0.0163)
	GFPI	0.0065(0.0042)	0.0106***(0.0030)	0.0097***(0.0021)
	Constant	−6.3229***(1.2175)	−2.1062**(0.8583)	−1.7011***(0.5887)
	Pseudo R^2	0.29	0.38	0.53

Standard errors in parenthesis. *, **, and *** signify 10%, 5% and 1% significance level, respectively.

Table 4.21 Robustness results for Turkey

Scales	Variables	25th Quantile	50th Quantile	75th Quantile
D1	MPR	1.4416***(0.5181)	0.9932**(0.4603)	0.8663(0.6183)
	HCE	3.14e-07(1.90e-07)	4.93e-07***(1.69e-07)	2.32e-07(2.27e-07)
	GFCF	−3.64e-07(2.20e-07)	−7.05e-07***(1.96e-07)	−3.64e-07(2.63e-07)
	USD	4.2328(3.7624)	6.7677**(3.3429)	5.2646(4.4898)
	GFPI	0.0404(0.0832)	0.0527(0.0740)	−0.0137(0.0993)
	Constant	−0.6973***(0.1135)	−0.0337(0.1009)	0.8174***(0.1355)
	Pseudo R^2	0.06	0.10	0.10
D2	MPR	−0.0485(0.5139)	0.3304(0.4450)	0.7217(0.6133)
	HCE	−3.64e-08(1.20e-07)	1.74e-07(1.04e-07)	1.20e-07(1.43e-07))
	GFCF	6.14e-08(1.33e-07)	−8.52e-08(1.15e-07)	−1.55e-07(1.58e-07)
	USD	1.3989(3.1454)	−0.0602(2.7240)	5.4572(3.7539)
	GFPI	0.1400*(0.0765)	0.0684(0.0662)	−0.0080(0.0913)
	Constant	−0.9393***(0.1653)	0.0312(0.1432)	0.8967***(0.1973)
	Pseudo R^2	0.06	0.05	0.03
D3	MPR	0.0335(0.3113)	0.0279(0.2655)	−0.0527(0.2925)
	HCE	6.89e-08(9.00e-08)	1.68e-07**(7.67e-08)	9.50e-08(8.45e-08)
	GFCF	7.02e-08(1.09e-07)	1.63e-08(9.32e-08)	3.43e-08(1.03e-07)
	USD	−2.2900(2.7873)	−3.3610(2.3775)	−2.4399(2.6186)
	GFPI	0.0406(0.0414)	0.0467(0.0354)	0.0442(0.0389)
	Constant	−0.8358***(0.1596)	−0.0699(0.1361)	0.7546**(0.1499)
	Pseudo R^2	0.06	0.07	0.05
D4	MPR	1.1181***(0.2122)	1.0734***(0.1781)	1.0234***(0.1183)
	HCE	1.67e-07(9.98e-08)	3.46e-07***(8.38e-08)	2.60e-07***(5.56e-08)
	GFCF	1.28e-07(1.26e-07)	−3.66e-08(1.06e-07)	−1.56e-09(7.01e-08)
	USD	−4.8417(3.4257)	−7.6064***(2.8762)	−4.1857**(1.9097)
	GFPI	−0.0136(0.0341)	−0.0253(0.0287)	−0.0271(0.0190)
	Constant	−0.8698***(0.1758)	0.2080(0.1476)	0.9327***(0.0980)
	Pseudo R^2	0.33	0.33	0.37
S4	MPR	0.4834***(0.0752)	0.6039***(0.0900)	0.6377***(0.0493)
	HCE	2.29e-07***(4.73e-08)	2.93e-07***(5.66e-08)	3.51e-07***(3.10e-08)
	GFCF	−2.72e-07***(6.15e-08)	−3.21e-07***(7.35e-08)	−3.40e-07***(4.03e-08)
	USD	−1.7287***(0.5935)	−1.1781*(0.7101)	−2.2081***(0.3889)
	GFPI	0.0667***(0.0155)	0.0579***(0.0185)	0.0401***(0.0102)
	Constant	−12.1738***(4.4282)	−21.2967***(5.2986)	−27.9894***(2.9018)
	Pseudo R^2	0.34	0.39	0.53

Standard errors in parenthesis. *, **, and *** signify 10%, 5% and 1% significance level, respectively.

5   Summary and conclusion

Introduction

This book looks at the monetary policy-food inflation nexus in the context of emerging and developing economies. Chapter one provides the general overview of the nexus, espouses on the state of the literature, the apparent gaps and then sets up an outline for the study. Chapter two navigates the nature of inflation targeting as practiced in the selected economies, their experiences and milestones achieved. Chapter three looks at the paths of world food prices, domestic food prices and the overall inflation. It then considers the implications of the paths of these series for the conduct of monetary policy. Chapter four is the empirical chapter. It looks at the theoretical and the empirical literature, the methodology, empirical findings and the robustness checks. The summary of the said findings is presented in section 5.2.

Summary of findings

This section presents the summary of the empirical results. Given that the estimations were done separately for each country, the summary is provided on the results obtained for each country.

Brazil

Monetary policy exerts a positive impact on food prices at scales D3 and D4. At scale D3, the monetary policy effect is statistically significant only at the 25th quantile. At scale D4, the positive monetary policy effect on food prices is statistically significant across all the quantiles. Real gross domestic product has a negative effect on food prices at scale D1, and the said effect is statistically significant across all the quantiles. At scale D2, the effect of real gross domestic product on food prices is

DOI: 10.4324/9781003195368-5

negative and statistically significant only at the 25th quantile. At scale D3, the effect of gross domestic product on food prices is positive but statistically significant only at the 25th quantile. At scale D4, the effect of the real gross domestic product is positive but significant at the 25th and the 75th quantiles. Exchange rate and the global food prices exert a positive impact on food prices at scale D4 and across all the quantiles.

Chile

At scale D1, the monetary policy effect on food prices is positive but statistically significant only at the 25th quantile. At scale D2, the monetary policy effect on food prices is positive but significant statistically at the median. At scale D3, the monetary policy effect on food prices is not statistically significant. At scale D4, the monetary policy effect on food prices is positive and statistically significant at all the quantiles of food inflation. The effect of the real gross domestic product on food prices at scale D1, although very marginal, is negative and a statistically significant across all the quantiles. The exchange rate effect on food prices at the same scale (D1) is positive and statistically significant at the 25th and 75th quantiles. The changes in global food prices exert statistically significant effect on domestic prices in Chile over the short-term horizon of two-to-four months (scale D1). At scale D2, the effect of the real gross domestic product on food prices is negative and statistically significant across all the quantiles. The effect of the exchange rate on food prices at scale D2 is also positive and statistically significant at all the quantiles. The effect of global food prices is positive but statistically significant at the 25th and 75th quantiles. At scale D3, the output effect on food prices is negative and statistically significant at all the quantiles. Similarly, the effect of exchange rate is also positive and statistically significant at the 25th and 75th quantiles.

Colombia

Monetary policy effect on food prices is mixed. Over the short horizon (scale D1 or two-to-four-month horizon), monetary policy impact on food prices is negative but statistically significant only at the 75th quantile. From scales D2 to D4, however, the monetary policy effect on food prices is positive and statistically significant. At scale D2, the monetary policy effect on food prices is positive but significant statistically only at the 25th quantile. At scale D3, monetary policy effect on food prices is positive and statistically significant across all the quantiles. Similarly, the effect of monetary policy at scale D4 on food prices is positive and statistically significant across all the quantiles. At scales D1, D3 and D4, the effect of the real gross domestic product on food prices in Colombia is negative but statistically significant across all the quantiles at D1, at the median at D3 and the 25th quantile at D4. For the exchange rate effect on food prices, it is negative but significant statistically only at the 25th quantile at scale D1. On the effect of global food prices on domestic food prices in Colombia, it is found that the effect is negative at scales D2, D3 and D4. At scale D2, the negative effect of global food prices is statistically significant only at the 25th quantile. At scale D3, the effect of global food prices on domestic food prices is significant only at the median. At scale D4, global food prices exert statistically significant impact on domestic prices in Colombia only at the 25th quantile.

Ghana

Monetary policy effect on food prices in Ghana is found to be positive and statistically significant only at the 75th quantile at scale D3. At scale D4, the monetary policy effect on food prices is positive and statistically significant across all the quantiles. It is found that the effect of global food prices on domestic food prices in Ghana is mixed. At scales D1 and D3, the effect is negative but positive at scales D2 and D4. At scales D1 and D2, the effect is significant only at the 75th quantile. At scale D3, global food prices exert a statistically significant positive impact on food prices only at the median. At scale D4, the effect is significant across all the quantiles.

Hungary

In Hungary, the results show that the effect of monetary policy on food inflation is positive (destabilising) and statistically significant at all the quantiles over the longer horizons or D3 and D4 scales. The destabilization is even greater over the longer horizons (scale D4). The long-term trend (S4) also shows a positive relationship between monetary policy and food prices. The real gross domestic product exerts a positive effect on food prices in Hungary at all the scales, although the effect is marginal across the quantiles. The findings also show that the global food prices impact domestic food prices positively in Hungary at all the scales. At scale D1, the positive effect is significant only at the median. At scale D2, the positive effect of the global food prices is significant at the 25th and 50th quantiles. At scales D3 and D4, global food prices exert a statistically significant positive effect on domestic food prices across all the quantiles.

Indonesia

Monetary policy effect on food inflation in Indonesia is found to be mixed. At scale D2, the monetary policy effect is positive but statistically significant at the 25th and 50th quantiles only. At scale D3, the monetary policy tightening exerts a negative effect on food prices but only statistically significant at the 50th and 75th quantiles. At scale D4, monetary policy tightening exerts a positive effect on food inflation at the 25th and 50th quantiles. The real gross domestic product exerts a positive effect on food prices in Indonesia at the 25th and 50th quantiles at scale D2. The exchange rate also exerts a positive effect on food prices at scale D2. Similarly at scale D3, the exchange rate impacts food prices positively in Indonesia across all the quantiles. Meanwhile, the global food prices exert a negative effect on domestic food prices in Indonesia across all the quantiles at scale D3. At scale D4, real gross domestic product impacts food prices positively across all quantiles. The exchange rate of the Rupiah to the Dollar also exerts a positive effect on food prices across all the quantiles. Moreover, global food prices impact domestic prices positively at the median and the 75th quantile.

Mexico

The results on Mexico show that monetary policy exerts a positive impact on food inflation over the long horizon (D4). At that scale, monetary policy effect is positive and statistically significant across all the quantiles. The long-term trend (S4) also indicates that monetary policy exerts a positive and significant effect on food prices across all the quantiles. Real gross domestic product impacts food prices negatively at scales D1 and D2 but only significantly so at the 75th quantile at both scales. At scale D4, real gross domestic product impacts food inflation negatively at both the median and the 75th quantile. Global food prices impact domestic food prices in Mexico negatively but the effect is statistically significant at the 25th quantile and the median at scale D2. The exchange rate of the Mexican Peso to the United States Dollar impacts food prices positively but only at the 25th quantile at scale D2.

Russia

Turning to Russia, the results show that monetary policy effect on food inflation is positive and significant at various quantiles at all the scales (D1 to D4). At scale D1, the monetary policy effect on food prices is positive but statistically significant only at the median. At scale D2, monetary policy's impact on food inflation is positive but statistically significant only at the 75th quantile. At scale D3, the positive monetary policy effect on food prices is statistically significant at the median and the 75th quantile. At scale D4 (longer horizon), the positive monetary policy effect on food prices magnifies and is statistically significant across all the quantiles. The effect of real gross domestic product on food prices is negative and statistically significant at scales D1 to D3. At scale D2, the exchange rate of the Russian Ruble against the United States Dollar has a positive effect on food prices but statistically significant only at the median. Global food prices exert a positive impact on domestic food prices in Russia at scales D3 and D4. At scale D3, the effect of global food prices on the domestic food prices is statistically significant at all quantiles. At scale D4, the effect is statistically significant across all the quantiles.

South Africa

For South Africa, it is found that monetary policy effect on food inflation is positive and statistically significant at scale D2 and specifically at the median. At scale D4, monetary policy exerts a positive impact on food prices across all the quantiles. The long-term trend (S4) also shows that monetary policy exerts a positive impact on food prices in South Africa. At scales D3 and D4, the effect of real gross domestic product on food inflation is negative and significant statistically across all quantiles. The exchange rate of the South African Rand to the United States Dollar exerts a positive effect on food prices in South Africa at scale D3. Meanwhile, the effect of the global food prices on the domestic food prices in South Africa at that scale (D3) is also positive but significant statistically only at the median. At scale D4, the exchange rate exerts a positive impact on food prices across all the quantiles. Global food prices also impact domestic food prices positively across all the quantiles at scale D4.

Turkey

Monetary policy effect on food prices at scale D1 in Turkey is positive but statistically significant only at the 25th quantile. Over the long medium-term horizon (scales D2 and D3), monetary policy effect on food prices in Turkey is statistically not significant. Over the long-term horizon (scale D4), the monetary policy effect on food prices is positive and statistically significant at all the quantiles of food inflation. The long-term trend (S4) also shows that the monetary policy effect on food prices is positive and statistically significant at all the quantiles. The effect of the real gross domestic product on food inflation in Turkey is mixed. At scale D2, real gross domestic product impacts food prices negatively but statistically significant only at the 75th quantile. At scales D3 and D4, real gross domestic product exerts a positive effect on food prices in Turkey. At scale D1, the exchange rate of the Turkish Lira to the United States Dollars exerts a positive effect on food prices but statistically significant only at the 75th quantile. At scale D2, the exchange rate impacts food prices positively at the median and the 75th quantile. At scale D4 however, exchange rate negatively impacts food prices across all the quantiles. Global food prices exert a negative impact on domestic food prices in Turkey at the median and the 75th quantile in scale D4.

Conclusion and recommendations

Much as literature on monetary policy-food inflation nexus is growing, fundamental limitations still linger. What makes food prices a major concern for monetary policy authorities is its underlying variability (volatilities) which minimises the accuracy of inflation forecasts; breeds uncertainty in the conduct of monetary policy; destabilise planning and income of farmers/producers and derail economic welfare for the poor in particular. Surprisingly, existing studies have tended to use models that completely ignore this all-important characteristic of food prices. Additionally, the approaches deployed fail to address the frequency of food price changes and deviations from the trend which are even more ruinous to inflation forecasting accuracy and engenders uncertainties in the conduct of monetary policy. Importantly, all the existing studies have been situated exclusively in time domain which ignores the fact that monetary policy authorities have distinct objectives over distinct horizons and frequencies. Indeed, Aguiar-Conraria et al. (2018) argue that monetary policy effect over distinct horizons and especially cyclical frequencies are crucial for policymakers, given the distinct impact on social welfare over these different frequencies.

This book overcomes these limitations in the literature by adopting an approach that situates the monetary policy-food inflation nexus in time and frequency domains. The wavelet-based quantile regressions are used to capture deviations of food prices from their trend and the accompanying monetary policy effect in stabilising such variabilities across distinct frequencies over time. The approach also helps in capturing monetary policy effect on food prices at high, medium and low episodes of food inflation.

The results show that the effect of monetary policy on food prices for the selected countries is mixed. While monetary policy exerts a positive impact on food prices over different horizons and distinct quantiles in Brazil, Chile, Ghana, Hungary, Mexico, Russia, South Africa and Turkey, monetary policy effect on food prices in Colombia and Indonesia are mixed. The results in these two countries differ across scales and quantiles. In Colombia, monetary policy delivers stability on food prices only over the short horizon or scale D1 (two-to-four-month horizon). At higher scales (D2 to D4) or longer horizons, the monetary policy effects on food prices in Colombia is positive. For Indonesia, food price stability is exacted by monetary policy over the two middle scales (D2 and D3). At the highest scale (D4), monetary policy restrictions engender destabilization in food prices. Given the dominance of food in the consumption baskets of emerging and developing economies and the high poverty levels, complementary fiscal and monetary policies would suit the situation of these countries better. Although the current study benefited from a more nuanced information on the monetary policy-food inflation nexus for the respective countries, future studies can consider a panel study to provide insights on common dynamics of emerging and developing countries.

Reference

Aguiar-Conraria, L., Martins, M. M., & Soares, M. J. (2018). Estimating the Taylor rule in the time-frequency domain. *Journal of Macroeconomics, 57*, 122–137.

Index